Important Instruc

Students, Parents, and Teachers can use the URL or QR code provided below to access Lumos back to school refresher online assessment. Please note that this assessment is provided in the Online format only.

URL
Visit the URL below and place the book access code
http://www.lumoslearning.com/a/tedbooks
Access Code: BS67M-47895-P
OR **Scan the QR code with your Smartphone**

Lumos Learning
Developed by Expert Teachers

Lumos Back-to-School Refresher tedBook - Grade 7 Math, Back to School book to address Summer Slide designed for classroom and home use

Contributing Author   - Renee Bade
Contributing Author   - Kimberly G
Executive Producer   - Mukunda Krishnaswamy
Designer and Illustrator - Devraj Dharmaraj

First Edition - 2020

NGA Center/CCSSO are the sole owners and developers of the Common Core State Standards, which does not sponsor or endorse this product. © Copyright 2010. National Governors Association Center for Best Practices and Council of Chief State School Officers.

ISBN-13: 978-1-081937-55-3

Printed in the United States of America

For permissions and additional information contact us

Lumos Information Services, LLC
PO Box 1575, Piscataway, NJ 08855-1575
http://www.LumosLearning.com

Email: support@lumoslearning.com
Tel: (732) 384-0146
Fax: (866) 283-6471

Lumos Learning
Developed by Expert Teachers

Table of Contents

INTRODUCTION

This book is specifically designed to help diagnose and remedy Summer Learning Loss in students who are starting their seventh grade classes. It provides a comprehensive and efficient review of 6th Grade Math standards through an online assessment. Before starting seventh grade instruction, parents/teachers can administer this online test to their students. After the students complete the test, a standards mastery report is immediately generated to pinpoint any proficiency gaps. Using the diagnostic report and the accompanying study plan, students can get targeted remedial practice through lessons included in this book to overcome any Summer learning loss.

Addressing the Summer slide during the first few weeks of a new academic will help students have a productive seventh grade experience.

The online program also gives your student an opportunity to briefly explore various standards that are included in the 7th grade curriculum.

Some facts about Summer Learning Loss
- Students often lose an average of 2 and ½ months of math skills
- Students often lose 2 months of reading skills
- Teachers spend at least the first 4 to 5 weeks of the new school year reteaching important skills and concepts

Lumos Learning Back-To-School Refresher Methodology
The following graphic shows the key components of the Lumos back-to-school refresher program.

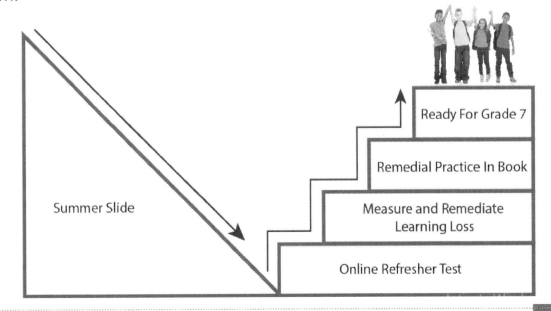

Chapter 1
Assess Summer Learning Loss

Step 1: Assess Online Diagnostic Assessment

Use the URL and access code provided below or scan the QR code to access the Diagnostic assessment and get started. The online diagnostic test helps to measure the summer loss and remediate loss in an efficient and effective way.

After completing the test, your student will receive immediate feedback with detailed reports on standards mastery. With this report, use the next section of the book to design a practice plan for your student to overcome the summer loss.

URL	QR Code
Visit the URL below and place the book access code **http://www.lumoslearning.com/a/tedbooks** **Access Code: BS67M-47895-P**	

Step 2: Review the Personalized Study Plan Online

After you complete the online practice test, access your individualized study plan from the table of contents (Figure 2)

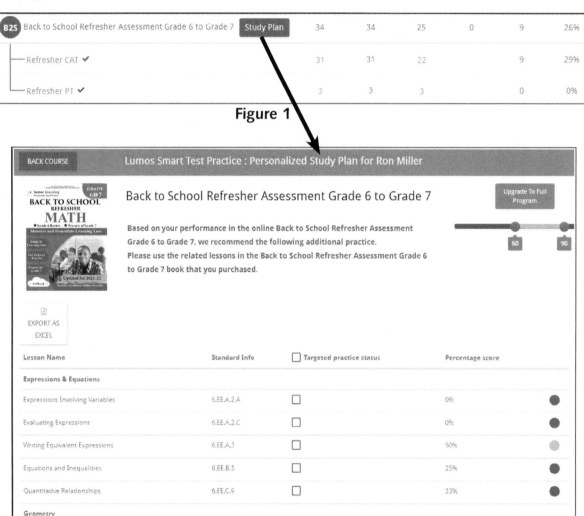

B2S Back to School Refresher Assessment Grade 6 to Grade 7 Study Plan	34	34	25	0	9	26%
Refresher CAT ✔	31	31	22		9	29%
Refresher PT ✔	3	3	3		0	0%

Figure 1

BACK COURSE   Lumos Smart Test Practice : Personalized Study Plan for Ron Miller

Back to School Refresher Assessment Grade 6 to Grade 7

Based on your performance in the online Back to School Refresher Assessment Grade 6 to Grade 7, we recommend the following additional practice.
Please use the related lessons in the Back to School Refresher Assessment Grade 6 to Grade 7 book that you purchased.

Upgrade To Full Program

EXPORT AS EXCEL

Lesson Name	Standard Info	☐ Targeted practice status	Percentage score	
Expressions & Equations				
Expressions Involving Variables	6.EE.A.2.A	☐	0%	●
Evaluating Expressions	6.EE.A.2.C	☐	0%	●
Writing Equivalent Expressions	6.EE.A.3	☐	50%	●
Equations and Inequalities	6.EE.B.5	☐	25%	●
Quantitative Relationships	6.EE.C.9	☐	33%	●
Geometry				

Figure 2

Step 3: Remediate Summer Learning Loss

Using the information provided in the study plan report, complete the targeted practice using the appropriate lessons in this book to overcome Summer learning loss. Using the Lesson Name, find the appropriate practice lessons in this book and answer the questions provided. After completing the practice in the book you can mark the progress in your study plan as shown the figure 2. Please use the answer key and detailed answers provided for each lesson to gain further understanding of the learning objective.

Ratios & Proportional Relationships

6.RP.A.1 Expressing Ratios

1. The little league team called the Hawks has 7 brunettes, 5 blonds, and 2 red heads. The entire little league division that the Hawks belong to has the same ratio of redheads to everyone else. What is the total number of redheads in that division if the total number of players is 126?

   Ⓐ 9
   Ⓑ 14
   Ⓒ 18
   Ⓓ 24

2. Barnaby decided to count the number of ducks and geese flying south for the winter. The first day he counted 175 ducks and 63 geese. What is the ratio of ducks to the total number of birds flying overhead in simplest terms?

   Ⓐ 175:63
   Ⓑ 175:238
   Ⓒ 25:9
   Ⓓ 25:34

3. Barnaby decided to count the number of ducks and geese flying south for the winter. The first day he counted 175 ducks and 63 geese. By the end of migration, Barnaby had counted 4,725 geese. If the ratio of ducks to geese remained the same (175 to 63), how many ducks did he count?

   Ⓐ 13,125
   Ⓑ 17,850
   Ⓒ 10,695
   Ⓓ 14,750

4. Barbara was baking a cake and could not find her tablespoon measure. The recipe calls for $3\frac{1}{3}$ tablespoons. Each table spoon measure 3 teaspoon. How many teaspoons must Barbara use in order to have the recipe turn out all right?

   Ⓐ 3
   Ⓑ 6
   Ⓒ 9
   Ⓓ 10

5. **Write the ratio that correctly describes the number of white stars compared to the number of gray stars. Write your answer in the box below.**

6.RP.A.2 Unit Rates

1. The Belmont race track known as "Big Sandy" is 1½ miles long. In 1973, Secretariat won the Belmont Stakes race in 2 minutes and 30 seconds. Assuming he ran on "Big Sandy", what was his unit speed?

   Ⓐ 30 mph
   Ⓑ 40 mph
   Ⓒ 36 mph
   Ⓓ 38 mph

2. If 1 pound of chocolate creams at Philadelphia Candies costs $7.52. How much does that candy cost by the ounce?

   Ⓐ 48¢ per oz.
   Ⓑ 47¢ per oz.
   Ⓒ 75.2¢ per oz.
   Ⓓ 66¢ per oz.

3. If Carol pays $62.90 to fill the 17-gallon gas tank in her vehicle and she can drive 330 miles on one tank of gas, about how much does she pay per mile to drive her vehicle?

   Ⓐ $0.37
   Ⓑ $3.70
   Ⓒ $0.19
   Ⓓ $0.01

4. A 13 ounce box of cereal cost $3.99. What is the unit price per pound?

   Ⓐ about $1.23
   Ⓑ about $2.66
   Ⓒ about $4.30
   Ⓓ about $4.91

5. 1 bag of apples costs $3.20. The cost of one apple is _____.

6.RP.A.3 Solving Real World Ratio Problems

1. On Monday, 6 out of every 10 people who entered a store purchased something. If 1,000 people entered the store on Monday, how many people purchased something?

   Ⓐ 6 people
   Ⓑ 60 people
   Ⓒ 600 people
   Ⓓ 610 people

2. If a pair of pants that normally sells for $51.00 is now on sale for $34.00, by what percentage was the price reduced?

   Ⓐ 30%
   Ⓑ 60%
   Ⓒ 33.33%
   Ⓓ 66.67%

3. If Comic Book World is taking 28% off the comic books that normally sell for $4.00, how much money is Kevin saving if he buys 12 comic books during the sale?

   Ⓐ $28
   Ⓑ $12
   Ⓒ $13.44
   Ⓓ $14.58

4. Eric spends 45 minutes getting to work and 45 minutes returning home. What percent of the day does Eric spend commuting?

   Ⓐ 6.25%
   Ⓑ 7.8%
   Ⓒ 5.95%
   Ⓓ 15%

5. Look at the ratio information found in the table below. Complete the table by correctly filling in the missing information.

Feet	Yards
3	1
6	
	3
15	5
24	

6.RP.A.3.B Solving Unit Rate Problems

1. Geoff goes to the archery range five days a week. He must pay $1.00 for every ten arrows that he shoots. If he spent $15.00 this week on arrows what is the average number of arrows Geoff shot per day?

   Ⓐ 3 arrows
   Ⓑ 30 arrows
   Ⓒ 45 arrows
   Ⓓ 75 arrows

2. Julia made 7 batches of cookies and ate 3 cookies. There were 74 cookies left. Which expression can be used to determine the average number of cookies per batch?

   Ⓐ 74÷7
   Ⓑ (74+7)÷3
   Ⓒ $\dfrac{74 + 3}{7}$
   Ⓓ $\dfrac{74}{3} \times 7$

3. Lars delivered 124 papers in 3 hours. How long did it take Lars to deliver one paper?

   Ⓐ 1 minute
   Ⓑ 1 minute and 27 seconds
   Ⓒ 1 minute and 45 seconds
   Ⓓ 2 minutes and 3 seconds

4. Mr. and Mrs. Fink met their son Conrad at the beach. Mr. and Mrs. Fink drove 462 miles on 21 gallons of fuel. Conrad drove 456 miles on 12 gallons of fuel. How many more miles per gallon does Conrad's car get than Mr. and Mrs. Fink's car?

   Ⓐ 6 mpg
   Ⓑ 22 mpg
   Ⓒ 16 mpg
   Ⓓ 38 mpg

5. John paid $15 for 3 cheeseburgers. What is the rate of one cheeseburger? Enter your answer in the box below.

   $

6.RP.A.3.C Finding Percent

1. Joshua brought 156 of his 678 Legos to Emily's house. What percentage of his Legos did Joshua bring?

   Ⓐ 4%
   Ⓑ 23%
   Ⓒ 30%
   Ⓓ 43%

2. At batting practice Alexis hit 8 balls out of 15 into the outfield. Which equation below can be used to determine the percentage of balls hit into the outfield?

   Ⓐ $\dfrac{15}{8} = \dfrac{x}{100}$

   Ⓑ $\dfrac{15}{100} = \dfrac{x}{8}$

   Ⓒ $8x = (100)(15)$

   Ⓓ $\dfrac{15}{8} = \dfrac{100}{x}$

3. Nikki grows roses, tulips, and carnations. She has 78 flowers of which 32% are roses. Approximately how many roses does Nikki have?

   Ⓐ 18 roses
   Ⓑ 25 roses
   Ⓒ 28 roses
   Ⓓ 41 roses

4. Victor took out 30% of his construction paper. Of this, Paul used 6 sheets, Allison used 8 sheets and Victor and Gayle used the last ten sheets. How many sheets of construction paper did Victor not take out?

   Ⓐ 24 sheets
   Ⓑ 50 sheets
   Ⓒ 56 sheets
   Ⓓ 80 sheets

5. **The following items were bought on sale. Complete the missing information.**

Item Purchased	Original Price	Amount of Discount	Amount Paid
Video Game	$80	20%	
Movie Ticket	$14		$11.20
Laptop	$1,000		$750
Shoes	$55.00	10%	$49.5

6.RP.A.3.D Measurement Conversion

1. Quita recorded the amount of time it took her to complete her chores each week for a month; 1 hour 3 minutes, 1 hour 18 minutes, 55 minutes, and 68 minutes. How many hours did Quita spend doing chores during the month?

   Ⓐ 3.8 hours
   Ⓑ 4.24 hours
   Ⓒ 4.4 hours
   Ⓓ 5.7 hours

2. Lamar can run 3 miles in 18 minutes. At this rate, how much distance he can run in one hour?

   Ⓐ 0.9 mph
   Ⓑ 1.1 mph
   Ⓒ 10 mph
   Ⓓ 21 mph

3. A rectangular garden has a width of 67 inches and a length of 92 inches. What is the perimeter of the garden in feet?

   Ⓐ 13.25 feet
   Ⓑ 26.5 feet
   Ⓒ 31.8 feet
   Ⓓ 42.8 feet

4. Pat has a pen pal in England. When Pat asked how tall his pen pal was he replied, 1.27 meters. If 1 inch is 2.54 cm, how tall is Pat's pen pal in feet and inches?

   Ⓐ 3 feet 11 inches
   Ⓑ 4 feet 2 inches
   Ⓒ 4 feet 6 inches
   Ⓓ 5 feet exactly

5. How many meters are there in 16 kilometers? Circle the correct answer choice.

   Ⓐ 1.6 m
   Ⓑ 1,600 m
   Ⓒ 16,000 m
   Ⓓ 160 m

Ratios & Proportional Relationships

Answer Key
&
Detailed Explanations

6.RP.A.1 Expressing Ratios

Question No.	Answer	Detailed Explanations
1	C	Set up the proportion: $\frac{2}{14}=\frac{x}{126}$, $\frac{1}{7}=\frac{x}{126}$, cross multiply to get $7x = 126$, then divide by 7 and $x = 18$.
2	D	The total number of birds is 175+63 = 238. Thus, the ratio of ducks to total birds is 175:238. To find the ratio in simplest terms, divide by the GCF(175, 238) =7. The ratio in simplest terms is 25:34.
3	A	The ratio of ducks to geese is 175:63. To find how many ducks, set up a proportion of $\frac{175}{63} = \frac{x}{4,725}$. Find the cross products: 175*4,725 = 63*x 826,875 = 63x Divide both sides by 63 x = 13,125
4	D	There are 3 teaspoons to each tablespoon. Thus $3 * \frac{10}{3} = 10$ teaspoons.
5	4:5	4:5. There are 4 white stars and 5 gray stars.

6.RP.A.2 Unit Rates

Question No.	Answer	Detailed Explanations
1	C	Set up a ratio of distance/time. Here, the ratio would be $\frac{1.5}{2.5}$ Then, create a proportion $\frac{1.5}{2.5} = \frac{x}{60}$, where 60 represents the number of minutes in an hour. Find the cross products: 1.5*60 = 2.5*x Simplify: 90 = 2.5x, Divide each side by 2.5 we get, x = 36.
2	B	There are 16 ounces in a pound, so $\frac{\$7.52}{16} = 47¢$
3	C	To find the cost of gas per mile: $\frac{\$62.90}{330}$ equals about $0.19 per mile. (Note: The capacity of the tank is extra information.)
4	D	$3.99/13 equals about $0.306 per ounce. Since there are 16 oz in a pound, multiply 16 by $0.306…, which equals about $4.91.
5	$ 0.40	To determine the unit rate for the cost of one apple, divide the cost of all the apples by the total number of apples: $3.20 ÷ 8 = .40 So, one apple has a unit rate cost of $.40.

6.RP.A.3 Solving Real World Ratio Problems

Question No.	Answer	Detailed Explanations
1	C	$\frac{6}{10} = \frac{x}{1000}$ x*10 = 6*1000 10x = 6000; Divide both sides by 10; x = 600
2	C	is/of = %/100 $\frac{34.00}{51.00} = \frac{x}{100}$ 34.00*100 = 51*x 3400 = 51x Divide both sides by 51 x = 66.67% This is the amount left to pay. 100%-66.67%=33.33% This is the amount the shirt was reduced by.
3	C	is/of = %/100 $\frac{x}{\$4.00} = \frac{28}{100}$ 4*28 = 100*x 112 = 100x Divide both sides by 100 x = $1.12; Then, multiply $1.12 * 12 = $13.44
4	A	is/of = x/100 use hours as your proportional rate 45 minutes + 45 minutes = 90 minutes or 1.5 hours $\frac{1.5}{24} = \frac{x}{100}$ 1.5*100 = 24*x 150 = 24x; Divide both sides by 24; x = 6.25%
5		<table><tr><th>Feet</th><th>Yards</th></tr><tr><td>3</td><td>1</td></tr><tr><td>6</td><td>2</td></tr><tr><td>9</td><td>3</td></tr><tr><td>15</td><td>5</td></tr><tr><td>24</td><td>8</td></tr></table> 1 yard = 3 feet Set up the proportion: yard/feet **(1) Let x be the number of yards in 6 feet.** $\frac{1}{3} = \frac{x}{6}$ 3x = 1 x 6 = 6 x = $\frac{6}{3}$ = 2 yards **(2) Let y be the number of feet in 3 yards** $\frac{1}{3} = \frac{3}{y}$ 1 x y = 3 x 3 = 9 or y = 9 **(3) Let z be the number of yards in 24 feet.** $\frac{1}{3} = \frac{z}{24}$ 3z = 1 x 24 = 24 z = $\frac{24}{3}$ = 8

6.RP.A.3.B Solving Unit Rate Problems

Question No.	Answer	Detailed Explanations
1	B	Find the unit rate for one day. Geoff shot 150 arrows ($15*10) $$\frac{150}{5} \text{ days} = \frac{x}{1}$$ 150*1=5*x 150 = 5x Divide both sides by 5 x = 30 arrows per day
2	C	Find the total number of cookies and divide by 7. The total number of cookies is 74 + 3 = 77. The number of batches is 7. So the total number of cookies per batch can be found using the expression (74 + 3)/7.
3	B	Find the unit rate for one paper. Change hours into minutes or 3 hrs = 3 * 60 mins $$\frac{180}{124} = \frac{x}{1}$$ 180*1=124*x 180 = 124x Divide both sides by 124 x = 1.45 minutes or 1 minutes and 27 seconds
4	C	Find the unit rate for both and compare. Fink's: 462 miles/21 gallons = 22 miles per gallon Conrad's: 456 miles/12 gallons = 38 gallons Difference: 38 − 22 = 16 gallons
5	5	Since 3 cheeseburgers cost $15, when you divide $15 by 3, you get cost of one cheeseburger, which is $5.

6.RP.A.3.C Finding Percent

Question No.	Answer	Detailed Explanations
1	B	156 of 178 legos in percentage would be $\frac{156}{178}$ x 100 = 23%
2	D	8 out 15 in terms of percentage would be $\frac{8}{15}$ x 100 = x. Hence, the correct answer is option D.
3	B	32% of the 78 flowers are roses. Therefore, number of roses = $\frac{32}{100}$ x 78 = 24.96 which is approximately equal to 25.
4	C	Total number of sheets used = 6 + 8 + 10 = 24 which is 30% of the total sheets (x). $\frac{30}{100}$ * x = 24 x = 80. Therefore, the number of sheets not taken out = 80−24 = 56.

Question No.	Answer	Detailed Explanations

Question No. 5

Item Purchased	Original Price	Amount of Discount	Amount Paid
Video Game	$80	20%	**$64**
Movie Ticket	$14	**20%**	$11.20
Laptop	$1,000	**25%**	$750
Shoes	$55.00	10%	$49.5

(1) Amount paid for video game = $64, Because $80 x 0.80 = $64 (20% discount means, one has to pay 80% of the original price. 80% = 0.80)

(2) Original price of the movie ticket = $14
Amount paid = $ 11.2
Discount = 14 - 11.2 = 2.8
% Discount /100 = Discount / original price
% Discount = 100 x (Discount / original price) = $100 \times (\frac{2.8}{14}) = \frac{280}{14}$
= 20%

(3) Discount for the Laptop = 1000 - 750 = 250
% Discount = 100 x (Discount / original price) = $100 \times (\frac{250}{1000})$
$= \frac{25000}{1000} = 25\%$

6.RP.A.3.D Measurement Conversion

Question No.	Answer	Detailed Explanations
1	C	Find the total number of minutes for the month: 1 h 3 m + 1 h 18 m + 55 m + 68 m = 63 m + 78 m + 55 m + 68 m = 264 minutes. There are 60 minutes in 1 hour. 264 min * ($\frac{1 \text{ hr}}{60 \text{ min}}$) = 4.4 hours
2	C	There are 60 minutes in 1 hour. 3 miles/18 minutes = x miles/60 minutes 3*60 = 18*x 180 = 18x Divide both side by 18 x = 10 miles per hour
3	B	Find the perimeter by adding all four sides of the garden: 67 + 67 + 92 + 92 = 318 in There are 12 inches in a foot. 318 in * ($\frac{1 \text{ foot}}{12 \text{ in}}$) = 26.5 feet
4	B	There are 100 cm in a meter and 2.54 cm in 1 inch. 1.27 meters * ($\frac{100 \text{ cm}}{1 \text{ m}}$) * ($\frac{1 \text{ in}}{2.54 \text{ cm}}$) = 50 inches 50 in / 12 in = 4.17 feet = 4 feet 2 inches
5	C	1000 meters/1 kilometer = x meters/16 kilometers 1000*16 = 1*x x = 16,000

The Number System

6.NS.A.1 Division of Fractions

1. **Calculate:** $2\dfrac{3}{4} \div \dfrac{11}{4} =$
   - (A) 1
   - (B) 2
   - (C) 3
   - (D) 4

2. **Calculate:** $\dfrac{7}{8} \div \dfrac{3}{4} =$
   - (A) $1\dfrac{1}{6}$

   - (B) 2

   - (C) $\dfrac{21}{32}$

   - (D) $\dfrac{5}{9}$

3. **Calculate:** $6\dfrac{3}{4} \div 1\dfrac{1}{8} =$
   - (A) $\dfrac{1}{6}$

   - (B) 4

   - (C) $5\dfrac{3}{4}$

   - (D) 6

4. **Fill in the blank.**

   $\dfrac{1}{2} \div 4 =$ _____?

6.NS.B.2 Division of Whole Numbers

1. **A marching band wants to raise $20,000 at its annual fundraiser. If they sell tickets for $20 a piece, how many tickets will they have to sell?**

   Ⓐ 500
   Ⓑ 10,000
   Ⓒ 100
   Ⓓ 1,000

2. **A classroom needs 3,200 paper clips for a project. If there are 200 paper clips in a package, how many packages will they need in all?**

   Ⓐ 160
   Ⓑ 1,600
   Ⓒ 18
   Ⓓ 16

3. **A homebuilder is putting new shelves in each closet he is building. He has 2,592 shelves in his inventory. If each closet needs 108 shelves, how many closets can he build?**

   Ⓐ 2.4
   Ⓑ 108
   Ⓒ 42
   Ⓓ 24

4. **Fill in the blank**

   $40,950 \div \text{\_\_\_\_} = 26$

6.NS.B.3 Operations with Decimals

1. **Which of these sets contains all equivalent numbers?**

   Ⓐ $\left\{0.75, \dfrac{3}{4}, 75\%, \dfrac{8}{12}\right\}$

   Ⓑ $\left\{0.100, \dfrac{5}{50}, 15\%, 0.010\right\}$

   Ⓒ $\left\{\dfrac{3}{8}, 35\%, 0.35, \dfrac{35}{100}\right\}$

   Ⓓ $\left\{\dfrac{9}{25}, 36\%, 0.360, \dfrac{18}{50}\right\}$

2. **Brian is mowing his lawn. He and his family have 7.84 acres. Brian mows 1.29 acres on Monday, 0.85 acres on Tuesday, and 3.63 acres on Thursday. How many acres does Brian have left to mow?**

   Ⓐ 2.70
   Ⓑ 20.7
   Ⓒ 2.07
   Ⓓ 0.207

3. **Hector is planting his garden. He makes it 5.8 feet wide and 17.2 feet long. What is the area of Hector's garden?**

   Ⓐ 9.976 square feet
   Ⓑ 99.76 square feet
   Ⓒ 99.76 feet
   Ⓓ 997.6 square feet

4. **Fill in the blank.**

   $7.1 \times 3.2 =$ _____

6.NS.B.4 Using Common Factors

1. Office A's building complex and the school building next door have the same number of rooms. Office A's building complex has floors with 5 one-room offices on each, and the school building has 11 classrooms on each floor. What is the fewest number of rooms that each building can have?

   Ⓐ 16
   Ⓑ 6
   Ⓒ 55
   Ⓓ $\frac{5}{11}$

2. How do you know if a number is divisible by 3?

   Ⓐ if the ones digit is an even number
   Ⓑ if the ones digit is 0 or 5
   Ⓒ if the sum of the digits in the number is divisible by 3 or a multiple of 3
   Ⓓ if the sum of the digits in the number is divisible by 2 and 3

3. Find the Greatest Common Factor (GCF) for 42 and 56.

   Ⓐ 21
   Ⓑ 14
   Ⓒ 7
   Ⓓ 2

4. Fill in the blank.

   The Greatest Common Factor (GCF) of 24, 36, and 48 is _____.

6.NS.C.5 Positive and Negative Numbers

1. The amount of snow on the ground increased by 4 inches between 4 p.m. and 6 p.m. If there was 6 inches of snow on the ground at 4 p.m. how many inches were on the ground at 6 p.m.?

    (A) 10 inches
    (B) 14 inches
    (C) 2 inches
    (D) 18 inches

2. The temperature at noon was 20° F. For the next 5 hours it dropped 2° F per hour. What was the temperature at 5:00 p.m.?

    (A) 15 degrees
    (B) 10 degrees
    (C) 5 degrees
    (D) 0 degrees

3. Tom enters an elevator that is in the basement, one floor below ground level. He travels three floors down to the parking level and then 4 floors back up. What floor does he end up on?

    (A) ground level
    (B) 2nd floor
    (C) 3rd floor
    (D) basement

4. On a number line, how far apart are -27 and 30? Write your answer in the box below.

6.NS.C.6.A Representing Negative Numbers

1. **−7.25 is between which two numbers on the number line?**

    Ⓐ −7 and −6
    Ⓑ −5 and −3
    Ⓒ −9 and −10
    Ⓓ −7 and −8

2. **What happens when you start at any number on a number line and add its additive inverse?**

    Ⓐ The number doubles.
    Ⓑ The number halves.
    Ⓒ The sum is zero.
    Ⓓ There is no movement.

3. **Which set of numbers would be found to the left of 4 on the number line?**

    Ⓐ {−1, 4, −5}
    Ⓑ {1, −4, −5}
    Ⓒ {1, 4, −5}
    Ⓓ {1, 4, 5}

4. **Circle the number with the highest value.**

    Ⓐ −17
    Ⓑ -28
    Ⓒ -36

6.NS.C.6.B Ordered Pairs

1. **In what Quadrant (I, II, III, IV) does the point (−0.75, −0.25) lie?**

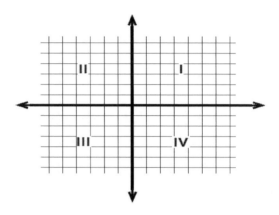

    Ⓐ Quadrant I
    Ⓑ Quadrant II
    Ⓒ Quadrant III
    Ⓓ Quadrant IV

2. **Point A, located at (10,−4), is reflected across the x-axis. What are the coordinates of the reflected point?**

    Ⓐ (−10, −4)
    Ⓑ (10, −4)
    Ⓒ (10, 4)
    Ⓓ (−10, 4)

3. **Point B, located at (6,3), is reflected across the y-axis. What are the coordinates of the reflected point?**

    Ⓐ (6, 3)
    Ⓑ (−6, −3)
    Ⓒ (6, −3)
    Ⓓ (−6, 3)

4. Circle the correct ordered pair for the point plotted below.

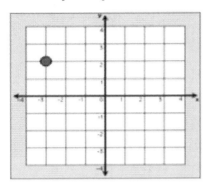

Ⓐ (3,2)

Ⓑ (-3,-2)

Ⓒ (-3,2)

6.NS.C.6.C Number Line & Coordinate Plane

1. **What number does the dot represent on the number line?**

Ⓐ −5
Ⓑ 0
Ⓒ 5
Ⓓ 10

2. Select the point located at (1,−2)

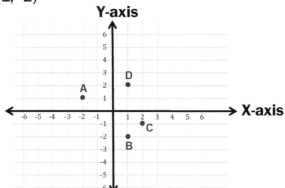

Ⓐ Point A
Ⓑ Point B
Ⓒ Point C
Ⓓ Point D

3. Select the point located at (−3,5)

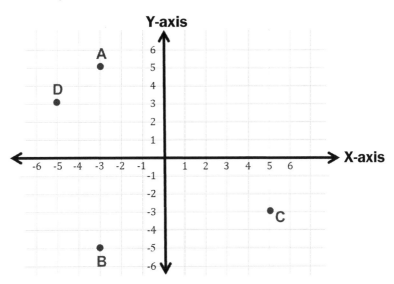

Ⓐ   Point A
Ⓑ   Point B
Ⓒ   Point C
Ⓓ   Point D

4. Circle the point that names the ordered pair (-9, -2).

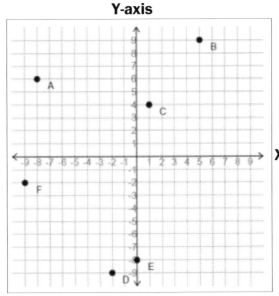

Point A   Point B   Point C

Point D   Point E   Point F

6.NS.C.7 Absolute Value

1. **Evaluate the following: |15 – 47| + 9 – |(–2)(–4) – 17|**

   Ⓐ 32
   Ⓑ –32
   Ⓒ 50
   Ⓓ 76

2. **Evaluate the following: 18 + 3 |6 – 25| – 11**

   Ⓐ 64
   Ⓑ 100
   Ⓒ 122
   Ⓓ 57

3. **Evaluate the following: 77 – |(–8)(3) + (–10)(4)|**

   Ⓐ 13
   Ⓑ 141
   Ⓒ –141
   Ⓓ –93

4. **Evaluate the following: 21 – |8 – (–5)(7)| – 54**

   Ⓐ –6
   Ⓑ 10
   Ⓒ –118
   Ⓓ –76

5. **What is the value of |14| – |–28|? Write your answer in the box below.**

6.NS.C.7.B Rational Numbers in Context

1. Doug and Sissy went scuba diving. Doug descended to –143 feet and Sissy descended to –134 feet. Who dove deeper?

   Ⓐ –134 > –143, so Sissy dove deeper.
   Ⓑ –134 < –143, so Doug dove deeper.
   Ⓒ –134 = –143, so neither one dove deeper as they descended the same amount.
   Ⓓ |–143|>|–134|, so Doug dove deeper.

2. At the annual town festival $\frac{4}{15}$ of the vendors sold outdoor items, 0.4 sold clothing or indoor items and $\frac{1}{3}$ sold food. Which of the following inequalities compares these three quantities accurately?

   Ⓐ $0.4 < \frac{4}{15} < \frac{1}{3}$

   Ⓑ $\frac{4}{15} > 0.4 > \frac{1}{3}$

   Ⓒ $0.4 > \frac{1}{3} > \frac{4}{15}$

   Ⓓ $\frac{1}{3} < \frac{4}{15} < 0.4$

3. A school of fish (S1) is spotted in the ocean at 15 feet below sea level. A second school (S2) of fish is spotted at $\frac{33}{3}$ feet below sea level. A third school (S3) of fish is spotted 11.5 feet below sea level. Order these numbers from deepest to shallowest. Note: The symbol > means deeper and < means shallower

   Ⓐ S1 < S3 < S2
   Ⓑ S3 < S2 < S1
   Ⓒ S1 > S3 > S2
   Ⓓ S3 < S1 < S2

4. Which temperature is hotter, 32 degrees or 56 degrees? Enter your answer in the box below.

6.NS.C.7.C Interpreting Absolute Value

1. **Ruth, who lives in Florida at an elevation of 30 meters, goes on a vacation to the Grand Cayman Islands, at an elevation of 24 meters, to go scuba diving at an elevation of −30 meters. Which elevation has the greatest absolute value?**

    Ⓐ 30 meters
    Ⓑ 24 meters
    Ⓒ −30 meters
    Ⓓ Both 30 meters and −30 meters have the greater absolute value.

2. **Connie, Julie, and Shelley's parents have encouraged them to save their money. Connie has an account balance of $215, Julie has −$100, and Shelley has −$250. Which inequality accurately represents the relative absolute values of each account.**

    Ⓐ |$215|<|−$100|<|−$250|
    Ⓑ |−$250|<|−$100|<|$215|
    Ⓒ |−$100|>|$215|>|−$250|
    Ⓓ |−$100|<|$215|<|−$250|

3. **The buoys on a certain lake mark the distance in meters from a center buoy. All buoys directly south are given negative numbers and all buoys directly north are given positive numbers. Betsy is located at buoy −6.2 and her brother Luis is located at buoy 6.5. Based on this information, which one of the following statements is not true.**

    Ⓐ Betsy is closer to the center buoy than Luis
    Ⓑ Luis is 6.5 meters from the center buoy.
    Ⓒ Luis is 0.2 meters farther from the center buoy than Betsy.
    Ⓓ Betsy is 12.7 meters from Luis.

4. **Sequence the numbers as they would fall on the number line in order from least to greatest. Enter the numbers in the correct answers in the boxes given below.**

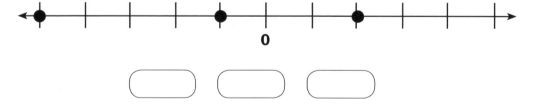

6.NS.C.7.D Comparisons of Absolute Value

1. The Casey quadruplets live in four different states. Dominik lives in Nantucket, Massachusetts at an elevation of 28 feet; Denzel lives in New Orleans, Louisiana at an elevation of 5.3 feet below sea level; Kaila lives in California near Death Valley at an elevation of 7 feet below sea level; and Malik lives in Nome, Alaska at an elevation of 20 feet. Who lives at the lowest elevation?

   Ⓐ Dominik
   Ⓑ Denzel
   Ⓒ Kaila
   Ⓓ Malik

2. One day in January the Casey quadruplets compared their location temperature.

Location	Temperature, °C
Nome, Alaska	14.9 below zero
Nantucket, Massachusetts	5.1 below zero
New Orleans, Louisiana	6 above zero
Death Valley, California	15 above zero

   Which location has the warmest temperature?

   Ⓐ Nome, Alaska
   Ⓑ Nantucket, Massachusetts
   Ⓒ New Orleans, Louisiana
   Ⓓ Death Valley, California

3. Sato, her brother Ichiro, and two friends, Aran and Mio, went to a festival. Before they could board any ride they had to be taller than the wooden height checker at each ride. At one ride Sato was 4 inches taller, Ichiro was 2 inches shorter, Aran was 6 inches taller and Mio was 2.5 inches shorter than the wooden height checker. Who is the shortest person?

   Ⓐ Sato
   Ⓑ Ichiro
   Ⓒ Aran
   Ⓓ Mio

4. Find the Value of $|12| - |-11| = $ _____?

6.NS.C.8 Coordinate Plane

1. **How many units does Yolanda need to walk from point C to point D? (Note: North is up on this map.)**

   Ⓐ 1 unit west and 7 units north
   Ⓑ 1 unit east and 7 units south
   Ⓒ 1 unit west and 7 units south
   Ⓓ 7 units west and 1 unit south

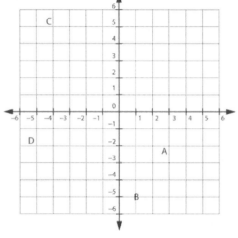

2. **What is the absolute value of Point D's coordinates?**

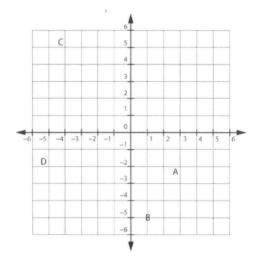

   Ⓐ (−5, 2)
   Ⓑ (5, −2)
   Ⓒ (−5, −2)
   Ⓓ (5, 2)

3. **There is a set of coordinates in Quadrant 4. The absolute value of x = 7. the absolute value of y = 3. What are the coordinates?**

   Ⓐ (−7, −3)
   Ⓑ (−3, −7)
   Ⓒ (7, −3)
   Ⓓ (−7, 3)

4. **What is the distance between these points shown on the picture? Enter the answer in the box given below.**

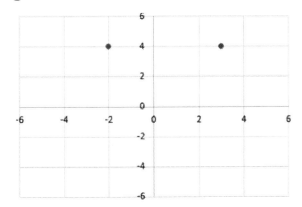

The Number System

Answer Key
&
Detailed Explanations

6.NS.A.1 Division of Fractions

Question No.	Answer	Detailed Explanation
1	A	The original problem is: $2\frac{3}{4} \div \frac{11}{4} =$ First convert the mixed fraction into improper fraction by using Numerator of the improper fraction = denominator of mixed fraction x whole part of the mixed fraction + numerator of the mixed fraction whereas the denominator of the improper fraction is same as that of the mixed fraction. So, $2\frac{3}{4} \div \frac{11}{4} = \frac{11}{4} \div \frac{11}{4} = 1$
2	A	The original problem is: $\frac{7}{8} \div \frac{3}{4} =$ Division of fractions can be obtained by multiplying the dividend with the reciprocal of the divisor. Thus, $\frac{7}{8} \div \frac{3}{4} = \frac{7}{8} \times \frac{4}{3} = \frac{28}{24} = \frac{7}{6} = 1\frac{1}{6}$
3	D	The original problem is: $6\frac{3}{4} \div 1\frac{1}{8} =$ First convert the mixed fractions into improper fraction by using Numerator of the improper fraction = denominator of mixed fraction x whole part of the mixed fraction + numerator of the mixed fraction whereas the denominator of the improper fraction is same as that of the mixed fraction. So, $6\frac{3}{4} \div 1\frac{1}{8} = \frac{27}{4} \div \frac{9}{8}$ Division of fractions can be obtained by multiplying the dividend with the reciprocal of the divisor. Thus, $\frac{27}{4} \div \frac{9}{8} = \frac{27}{4} \times \frac{8}{9}$ Cross factor out the GCF of 4 from 4 and 8 Cross factor out the GCF of 9 from 9 and 27 $\frac{3}{1} \times \frac{2}{1} = 6$

Question No.	Answer	Detailed Explanation
4	$\frac{1}{8}$	$\frac{1}{8}$. Because $\frac{1}{2} \div \frac{4}{1} = \frac{1}{2} \times \frac{1}{4} = \frac{1}{8}$

6.NS.B.2 Division of Whole Numbers

Question No.	Answer	Detailed Explanation
1	D	Let the number of tickets to be sold be n. Therefore, n * 20 = 20000 n = 20000 / 20 n = 1000
2	D	Number of packages(n) = Total number of clips required/Number of clips in one package n = 3200 / 200 n = 16
3	D	Number of closets that can be built(n) = Total number of shelves/ Number of shelves in each closet n = 2592 / 108 n = 24
4	1575	40950 / x = 26 x = 40950 / 26 x = 1575

6.NS.B.3 Operations With Decimals

Question No.	Answer	Detailed Explanation
1	D	The last set is the only set of numbers that are all equivalent. These numbers all have a decimal equivalent of 0.36.
2	C	1.29 + 0.85 + 3.63= 5.77 7.84 − 5.77 = 2.07 acres left to mow
3	B	Multiply the length by width to find the area. 5.8 * 17.2 Multiply the numbers and find the product. Then, count the decimal places in the factors. There is one decimal place for each factor or a total of two decimal places. Count two spaces from the right and put the decimal point in your answer. 5.8 * 17.2 = 99.76
4	22.72	Answer is 22.72 Because 71 x 32 = 2272. The factors have a total of 2 decimal places, therefore the answer should have 2 decimal places: 22.72

6.NS.B.4 Using Common Factors

Question No.	Answer	Detailed Explanation
1	C	Find the least multiple common to both numbers, starting with the greater number: 11: 11, 22, 33, 44, 55, 66, 77, 88... 5: 5, 10, 15, 20, 25, 30, 35, 40, 45, 50, 55 Stop when you get to the lowest multiple that is common to both. 55 is the LCM (lowest common multiple) of these two numbers, so each building could have 55 rooms.
2	C	When the sum of the digits in the number equals three or a multiple of 3, the number is divisible by 3. For example, 375 is divisible by 3 because $3 + 7 + 5 = 15$ Because 15 is a multiple of 3, the number is divisible by 3.
3	B	42: 1, 2, 3, 6, 7, 14, 21, 42 56: 1, 2, 4, 7, 8, 14, 28, 56
4	12	The Common Factors of 24, 36 and 48 are: 24: 1, 2, 3, 4, 6, 8, **12**, 24 36: 1, 2, 3, 4, 6, 9, **12**, 18, 36 48: 1, 2, 3, 4, 6, 8, **12**, 16, 24, 48 Hence, the Greatest Common Factor (GCF) is **12**.

6.NS.C.5 Positive and Negative Numbers

Question No.	Answer	Detailed Explanation
1	A	$6 + (+4) = 10$ inches
2	B	The change in temperature can be expressed as $5*(-2)$, or -10 degrees $20 + (-10) = 10$ degree F.
3	A	Call the basement 0, since the ground level would be considered the 1st floor. Tom's motion on the elevator can be described as $0 - 3 + 4 = 1$. He ends up on the 1st floor (ground level).
4	57	Answer is 57, because from 0 to 30 is a difference of 30 steps; 0 to -27 is a difference of 27 steps. Combined, this is a difference of 57 steps on the number line.

6.NS.C.6.A Representing Negative Numbers

Question No.	Answer	Detailed Explanation
1	D	-7.25 is less than -7 but greater than -8 so it would be the number found between -7 and -8.
2	C	Additive inverse of a given number has the same magnitude with opposite sign. $4 + (-4) = 0$
3	B	$\{1, -4, -5\}$ is the only set which would fall to the left of 4 on a number line. Any number larger than 4 would fall to the right on a number line and would not fit the criteria.
4	A	Answer is -17. Because it is only 17 numbers away from 0 whereas the other the other two options are 28 and 36 numbers away from 0. (Closest to 0 when dealing with negative numbers has the highest value).

6.NS.C.6.B Ordered Pairs

Question No.	Answer	Detailed Explanation
1	C	Quadrant III – In this quadrant both the x-coordinate and y-coordinate are negative.
2	C	When a point is reflected across the x-axis the x-coordinate remains the same and the y-coordinate changes sign. $(10, -4) \rightarrow (10, 4)$
3	D	When a point is reflected across the y-axis the y-coordinate remains the same and the x-coordinate changes sign. $(6, 3) \rightarrow (-6, 3)$
4	C	(-3,2) because the point is in the Quadrant II, where x - coordinate is negative and y - coordinate is positive. The given point is 2 units above x-axis so y coordinate = 2 and the point is 3 units to the left of y-axis so x coordinate = -3

6.NS.C.6.C Number Line & Coordinate Plane

Question No.	Answer	Detailed Explanation
1	C	Distance between -25 and +25 = 50. Distance between two consecutive ticks = 50/10 = 5. Therefore the dot represents the number 5.
2	B	An ordered pair is written in the format (x,y) where x is the first number and y is the second number. The point $(1,-2)$ is located 1 unit to the right (x-axis) and 2 units down (y-axis) from the origin. This is represented by Point B.
3	A	An ordered pair is written in the format (x,y) where x is the first number and y is the second number. The point $(-3,5)$ is located 3 units to the left (x-axis) and 5 units up (y-axis) from the origin. This is represented by Point A.
4	F	To find the point which is represented by the ordered pair (-9, -2), move 9 units from the origin to the left and 2 units down. From the graph we see that this represents point F.

6.NS.C.7 Absolute Value

Question No.	Answer	Detailed Explanation
1	A	$\|15 - 47\| + 9 - \|(-2)(-4) - 17\|$ $= \|-32\| + 9 - \|8 - 17\|$ $= 32 + 9 - \|-9\|$ $= 32 + 9 - 9$ $= 41\text{-}9$ $= 32$ Note: Absolute value (the value of $\|x\|$) is the value of a number without regard to its sign.
2	A	$18 + 3\|6 - 25\| - 11$ $= 18 + 3\|-19\| - 11$ $= 18 + 3(19) - 11$ $= 18 + 57 - 11$ $= 18 + 57 - 11$ $= 75 - 11$ $= 64$ Note: Absolute value (the value of $\|x\|$) is the value of a number without regard to its sign.

Question No.	Answer	Detailed Explanation
3	A	$77 - |(-8)(3) + (-10)(4)|$ $= 77 - |(-24) + (-40)|$ $= 77 - |-64|$ $= 77 - 64$ $= 13$ Note: Absolute value (the value of $|x|$) is the value of a number without regard to its sign.
4	D	$21 - |8 -(-5)(7)| - 54$ $= 21 - |8 - (-35)| - 54$ $= 21 - |8 + 35| - 54$ $= 21 - |43| - 54$ $= 21 - (43) - 54$ $= 21 + (-43) - 54$ $= -22 - 54$ $= -22 + (-54)$ $= -76$ Note: Absolute value (the value of $|x|$) is the value of a number without regard to its sign.
5	- 14	$|14| - |-28|$ $= 14 - 28 = -14$

6.NS.C.7.B Rational Numbers in Context

Question No.	Answer	Detailed Explanation
1	D	−143 means 143 feet below sea level. −134 feet means 134 feet below sea level. Therefore Doug dove deeper because he went further below sea level than Sissy.
2	C	Rewrite these three numbers all as decimals or fractions. $\frac{4}{15} = 0.27$ $0.4 = 0.4$ $\frac{1}{3} = 0.33$ Now compare: $0.4 > 0.33 > 0.27$ Now rewrite them in their original form: $0.4 > \frac{1}{3} > \frac{4}{15}$
3	C	15 feet below sea level $= -15$ feet $\frac{33}{3} = 11$ feet below sea level $= -11$ feet 11.5 feet below sea level $= -11.5$ feet The deepest school is the one with the greater negative magnitude. Therefore: -15 is deeper than -11.5 is deeper than -11 or S1 > S3 > S2.
4	56	The answer is 56 degrees. Comparing the 2 values, 32 or 56, 56 degrees would be hotter when compared to 32 degrees.

6.NS.C.7.C Interpreting Absolute Value

Question No.	Answer	Detailed Explanation
1	D	$\|30\| = 30$ $\|24\| = 24$ $\|-30\| = 30$ Therefore both 30 and -30 have the greater absolute value.
2	D	$\|215\| = \$215$ $\|-100\| = \$100$ $\|-250\| = \$250$ $100 < 215 < 250$ or $\|-100\| < \|215\| < \|-250\|$

Question No.	Answer	Detailed Explanation
3	C	True. Betsy is 6.2 meters away from the center buoy and Luis is 6.5 meters away. Betsy is closer by 0.3 meters. True. Luis is 6.5 meters from the center buoy. False. Betsy is 6.2 meters away from the center buoy and Luis is 6.5 meters away. Luis is 0.3 meters farther from the buoy. True. Betsy is 6.2 meters directly south of the center buoy which is 6.5 meters directly south of Luis therefore Betsy is 6.2 + 6.5 = 12.7 meters from Luis.
4		-5, -1, 2 because negative numbers fall to the left of the 0.

6.NS.C.7.D Comparisons of Absolute Value

Question No.	Answer	Detailed Explanation
1	C	Dominik: 28 feet Denzel: −5.3 feet (5.3 feet below sea level) Kaila: −7 feet (7 feet below sea level) Malik: 20 feet The lowest elevation is −7 feet where Kaila lives.
2	D	14.9 below zero = −14.9 5.1 below zero = −5.1 6 above zero = 6 15 above zero = 15 The warmest temperature is the greatest positive number or 15 degrees C in Death Valley, California.
3	D	Sato: +4 inches Ichiro: −2 inches Aran: +6 inches Mio: −2.5 inches The shortest person is Mio.
4	1	Answer is 1, because the absolute value of 12 is 12, and that of -11 is 11. So 12 - 11 = 1.

6.NS.C.8 Coordinate Plane

Question No.	Answer	Detailed Explanation
1	C	Point C is at $(-4, 5)$ and Point D is at $(-5, -2)$. That means that Yolanda has to walk 1 unit west (left) and 7 units south (down).
2	D	The coordinates of Point D are $(-5, -2)$. Absolute value is the positive value of a number. That means the absolute value is $(5, 2)$.
3	C	The x coordinate is listed first in a coordinate pair, and the y coordinate is listed second. The absolute value of a number is its positive value. In Quadrant IV, the x coordinate is positive and the y coordinate is negative. That makes the coordinates $(7, -3)$.
4	5	The coordinates of the point in the 1st quadrant are - $(3,4)$ and that of the point in 2nd quaadrant are $(-2,4)$. So the distance between these points will be $3-(-2) = 5$

Expressions & Equations

6.EE.A.1 Whole Number Exponents

1. **Simplify: $(b^2c)(bc^3)$**

   Ⓐ 3b/4
   Ⓑ 3b * 4
   Ⓒ b^3c^4
   Ⓓ bc

2. **Simplify: $(n^4x^2)^3$**

   Ⓐ 12n*6x
   Ⓑ $n^{12}x^6$
   Ⓒ $n^{43}x^{23}$
   Ⓓ n^7x^5

3. **Simplify: $7^4/7^2$**

   Ⓐ 7^6
   Ⓑ 7^3
   Ⓒ 7^2
   Ⓓ 7^4

4. **Simplify: $[(3^5)(3^2)]^4$**

   Ⓐ 3^{28}
   Ⓑ 3^{40}
   Ⓒ 3^{10}
   Ⓓ 3^{11}

5. **Find the numerical value of 8^4. Write your answer in standard form in the box.**

6.EE.A.2.A Expressions Involving Variables

1. For which of the following values of b does the expression 4b – 9 have a value between 90 and 100?

   Ⓐ b = 104
   Ⓑ b = 26
   Ⓒ b = 48
   Ⓓ b = 24

2. Evaluate the following when n = –4: [5n – 3n] + 2n

   Ⓐ b = 16
   Ⓑ b = –20
   Ⓒ b = –16
   Ⓓ b = 0

3. Translate the following: "Four times a number n is equal to the difference between that number and 10"

   Ⓐ 4n = 10 – n
   Ⓑ 4 + n = 10*n
   Ⓒ 4/n = n + 10
   Ⓓ 4n = n – 10

4. Which of the following represents the phrase "the quotient of 17 and q"? Select all the correct answers.

   Ⓐ q ÷ 17
   Ⓑ 17 ÷ q
   Ⓒ 17/q
   Ⓓ q/17

6.EE.A.2.B Identifying Expression Parts

1. **Which of the following describes the expression $4 \div (5 \times \frac{1}{2})$ accurately?**

   Ⓐ The quotient of 4 and $5\frac{1}{2}$

   Ⓑ divided by the quotient of 5 and $\frac{1}{2}$

   Ⓒ The quotient of 4 and the product of 5 and $\frac{1}{2}$

   Ⓓ The product of 5 and $\frac{1}{2}$ divided by 4.

2. **Which of the following describes the expression $(6+9) - 4$ accurately?**

   Ⓐ 4 subtracted from the sum of 6 and 9.
   Ⓑ The sum of 6 and 9 subtracted from 4.
   Ⓒ The difference of 6 and 9 less 4.
   Ⓓ The sum of the quantity of 6 plus 9 and 4.

3. **Which term has the smallest coefficient in the expression $8x^4 + \frac{7}{8}x^3 - 2x^2 + x$?**

   Ⓐ 1st term
   Ⓑ 2nd term
   Ⓒ 3rd term
   Ⓓ 4th term

4. _____ **is the same as $(3+1) + (3+1)$. Circle the correct answer choice.**

   Ⓐ $2(3+1)$
   Ⓑ $3(2+1)$
   Ⓒ $(3+1)^2$

6.EE.A.2.C Evaluating Expressions

1. Evaluate the following expression when v = −2 and w = 155: $6v^3 + \dfrac{4}{5}w$

    Ⓐ 17
    Ⓑ 68
    Ⓒ 76
    Ⓓ 172

2. Evaluate the following expression when c = −3 and d = 2: $\dfrac{6}{d} - 10c - c^4$

    Ⓐ −108
    Ⓑ −48
    Ⓒ 39
    Ⓓ 114

3. Use the formula $V = s^3$ to find the volume of a cube with a side length of 2 cm.

    Ⓐ 4 cm²
    Ⓑ 6 cm³
    Ⓒ 8 cm³
    Ⓓ 9 cm³

4. Circle the answer that fits the 'x' in this equation $\dfrac{1200}{x} = 30$.

    Ⓐ 4
    Ⓑ 40
    Ⓒ 400

6.EE.A.3 Writing Equivalent Expressions

1. **Simplify the following equation:**
   u + u + u + u − p + p + p − r = 55

   Ⓐ 4u + 2p − r = 55
   Ⓑ 4u + p − r = 55
   Ⓒ 4u − 3p + r = 55
   Ⓓ 4u − 3p − r = 55

2. **36x − 12 = 108 has the same solution(s) as _____ .**

   Ⓐ 3(3x − 12) = 108
   Ⓑ 12(3x −1) = 108
   Ⓒ 3(12x − 12) = 108
   Ⓓ 12(x−1) = 108

3. **Why is the expression 5(3x + 2) equivalent to 15x + 10?**

   Ⓐ The 5 has been divided into each term in parentheses.
   Ⓑ The 5 was distributed using the Distributive Property.
   Ⓒ The 5 was distributed using the Associative Property.
   Ⓓ The expressions are not equal.

4. **Which expression is equivalent to 5b − 9c − 2(4b + c)?**

   Ⓐ −3b + 7c
   Ⓑ −3b − 7c
   Ⓒ −3b − 11c
   Ⓓ −3b + 11c

5. **Write the correct equation for the following expression. 3 less than the product of 4 and 5.**

6.EE.A.4 Identifying Equivalent Expressions

1. **(800 + 444y)/4 is equivalent to:**

    Ⓐ 200 + 44y
    Ⓑ 800 + 111y
    Ⓒ 200 + 111y
    Ⓓ 200 − 111y

2. **5(19 −8y) is equivalent to:**

    Ⓐ 95 − 35y
    Ⓑ 95 + 40y
    Ⓒ 85 − 40y
    Ⓓ 95 − 40y

3. **The expression 3(26p − 7 + 14h) is equivalent to:**

    Ⓐ 78 − 21 + 42
    Ⓑ 78p + 21 + 42h
    Ⓒ 78p − 21 + 42
    Ⓓ 78p − 21 + 42h

4. **[(8y) + (8y) + (8y)] ÷ 2 = _____ . Simplify the expression and write the answer in the box.**

6.EE.B.5 Equations and Inequalities

1. **Which of the following correctly shows the number sentence that the following words describe?** *The square of the sum of 6 and b is greater than 10.*

   Ⓐ $(6 + b)^2 > 10$
   Ⓑ $6^2 + b^2 > 10$
   Ⓒ $(6 + b)^2 = 10$
   Ⓓ $(6 + b)^2 < 10$

2. **Which of the following correctly shows the number sentence that the following words describe?** *16 less than the product of 5 and h is 21.*

   Ⓐ $16 - 5h = 21$
   Ⓑ $5h - 16 = 21$
   Ⓒ $16 - (5 + h) = 21$
   Ⓓ $16 < 5h + 21$

3. **Which of the following correctly shows the number sentence that the following words describe?** *8 times the quantity 2x – 7 is greater than 5 times the quantity 3x + 9.*

   Ⓐ $8(2x) - 7 > 5(3x) + 9$
   Ⓑ $8(2x - 7) \geq 5(3x + 9)$
   Ⓒ $8(2x - 7) > 5(3x + 9)$
   Ⓓ $8(2x - 7) < 5(3x + 9)$

4. **Circle the answer that correctly represents "d" in this equation.**

   $3d + 4 > 17$

   Ⓐ 5
   Ⓑ 2
   Ⓒ 4

6.EE.B.6 Modeling with Expressions

1. Janie had 54 stamps. She gave away t stamps. She then got back twice as many as she had given away. Which expression shows how many stamps Janie has now?

   Ⓐ 54 – t
   Ⓑ 54 + t
   Ⓒ 54 – 2t
   Ⓓ 2t – 54

2. The library has 2,500 books. The librarian wants to purchase x more books for the library. The director decides to buy twice as many as the librarian requested. How many books will the library have if the director purchases the number of books he wants?

   Ⓐ 2,500 + x
   Ⓑ 2,500 + 2x
   Ⓒ 2,500 – x
   Ⓓ 2,500 – 2x

3. There are 24 boys and 29 girls (not including Claire) attending Claire's birthday party. Which equation shows how many cupcakes Claire needs to have so that everyone, including herself, will have a cupcake?

   Ⓐ 24 – 29 = c
   Ⓑ 24 + 29 = c
   Ⓒ 24 + 30 = c
   Ⓓ 24 + c = 29

4. Circle the answer that represents the statement 43 is greater than q correctly.

   Ⓐ q > 43
   Ⓑ 43 + q
   Ⓒ 43 > q

6.EE.B.7 Solving One-Step Equations

1. **Find the value of z:** $\dfrac{z}{5} = 20$

   Ⓐ 100
   Ⓑ 4
   Ⓒ 15
   Ⓓ 25

2. **Find the value of y:** $\dfrac{y}{3} = 12$

   Ⓐ 9
   Ⓑ 15
   Ⓒ 36
   Ⓓ 4

3. **Find the value of p:** $13 + p = 39$

   Ⓐ 3
   Ⓑ 26
   Ⓒ 507
   Ⓓ 52

4. **Find the value of *w*:** $6w = 54$

   Ⓐ 48
   Ⓑ 60
   Ⓒ 324
   Ⓓ 9

5. **Circle the answer that represents m correctly in the equation 4m = 16.**

   Ⓐ m = 4
   Ⓑ m = 3
   Ⓒ m = 12

6.EE.B.8 Representing Inequalities

1. "Three times the sum of six times a number and three is less than 27." is represented as _____.

   Ⓐ $6x + 3 < 27$
   Ⓑ $3(6)x + 3 > 27$
   Ⓒ $3(6x + 3) < 27$
   Ⓓ $6x + 3(3) < 27$

2. How would $x > 3$ be represented on a number line?

   Ⓐ The number line would show an open circle over three with an arrow pointing to the left.
   Ⓑ The number line would show an open circle over three with an arrow pointing to the right.
   Ⓒ The number line would show a closed circle over three with an arrow pointing to the right.
   Ⓓ The number line would show a closed circle over three with an arrow pointing to the left.

3. Amy and Joey each have jellybeans. The amount Amy has is 3 times the amount that Joey has. There are at least 44 jellybeans between them. Which inequality would help you figure out how many jellybeans Amy and Joey each have?

   Ⓐ $x + 3x \geq 44$
   Ⓑ $3x \geq 44$
   Ⓒ $3 + x \geq 44$
   Ⓓ $x + 3x \leq 44$

4. "A number divided by 5 is at most -23" is represented as _____.
   Write the inequality and explain.

6.EE.C.9 Quantitative Relationships

1. Penny planned a picnic for her whole family. It has been very hot outside, so she needs a lot of lemonade to make sure no one is thirsty. There are 60 ounces in each bottle. Penny purchased b bottles of lemonade. She wants to figure out the total number of ounces (o) of lemonade she has. Which equation should she use?

    Ⓐ b = 60(o)
    Ⓑ 60 = o x b
    Ⓒ 60(b) = o
    Ⓓ 60 = b ÷ o

2. Ethan is playing basketball in a tournament. Each game lasts 24 minutes. Ethan has 5 games to play. Which general equation could he use to help him figure out the total number of minutes that he played? Let t = the total time, g = the number of games, and m = the time per game.

    Ⓐ t = g + m
    Ⓑ t = g(m)
    Ⓒ t = g − m
    Ⓓ t = g ÷ m

3. The Spencers built a new house. They want to plant trees around their house. They want to plant 8 trees in the front yard and 17 in the backyard. The trees that the Spencer's want to plant cost $46 each. Could they use the equation t = c(n) where t is the total cost, c is the cost per tree, and n is the number of trees purchased, to figure out the cost to purchase trees for both the front and the back yards?

    Ⓐ No, because the variables represent only two specific numbers that will never change.
    Ⓑ Yes, because the variables represent only two specific numbers that will never change.
    Ⓒ No, because the variables can be filled in with any number.
    Ⓓ Yes, because the variables can be filled in with any number.

4. Sodas cost $1.25 at the vending machine. Complete the table to show the quantity and total cost of sodas purchased.

Day	Money Spent on Sodas	Sodas Purchased	Price per Soda
Monday		24	$1.25
Wednesday	$57.50		$1.25
Friday	$41.25		$1.25

Expressions & Equations

Answer Key
&
Detailed Explanations

6.EE.A.1 Whole Number Exponents

Question No.	Answer	Detailed Explanation
1	C	We know that $a^m*a^n = a^{(m+n)}$. Therefore, $(b^2c)(bc^3) = b^3c^4$
2	B	We know that $(a^m)^n = a^{m+n}$. Therefore, $(n^4x^2)^3 = n^{12}x^6$
3	C	We know that $a^m/a^n = a^{(m-n)}$. Therefore, $7^4/7^2 = 7^2$
4	A	We know that $a^m*a^n = a^{(m+n)}$ and $(a^m)^n = a^{mn}$. Therefore, $[3^5*3^2]^4 = [3^7]^4 = 3^{28}$
5	4096	$8^4 = 8 \times 8 \times 8 \times 8 = 4,096$

6.EE.A.2.A Expressions Involving Variables

Question No.	Answer	Detailed Explanation
1	B	When $b = 26$, $4b - 9 = 4(26) - 9 = 104 - 9 = 95$
2	C	When $n = -4$, the expression becomes: $= [5(-4) - 3(-4)] + 2(-4)$ $= [-20 - (-12)] - 8$ $= [-20 + 12] - 8$ $= [-8] - 8$ $= -16$ **Alternative Solution:** $[5n-3n]+2n = 2n + 2n = 4n = 4*(-4) = -16$
3	D	Four times a number n means to multiply the variable n by 4, 4n. is equal to means = the difference between a number and 10 means to write the subtraction as is, from left to right, so $n - 10$. Therefore, $4n = n - 10$
4	B & C	B and C, The order of the numbers should match the phrase.

6.EE.A.2.B Identifying Expression Parts

Question No.	Answer	Detailed Explanation
1	C	$(5 \times \frac{1}{2}) \rightarrow$ The product of 5 and $\frac{1}{2}$ $4 \div (5 \times \frac{1}{2}) \rightarrow$ The quotient of 4 and the product of 5 and $\frac{1}{2}$
2	A	$(6 + 9) \rightarrow$ The sum of 6 and 9 or 6 plus 9 $- 4 \rightarrow$ less 4 or 4 subtracted from $(6 + 9) - 4 = 4$ subtracted from the sum of 6 and 9
3	C	A coefficient is the number multiplied by a variable. In this expression there are four variable terms, $8x^4$, $\frac{7}{8}x^3$, $-2x^2$ and x. The coefficients are 8, $\frac{7}{8}$, -2 and 1. The value of the smallest coefficient is -2. Therefore the third term has the smallest coefficient.
4	A	A number or an expression added to itself is twice the number or expression.

6.EE.A.2.C Evaluating Expressions

Question No.	Answer	Detailed Explanation	
1	C	$6v^3 + \frac{4}{5}w$	Original equation
		$6(-2)^3 + \frac{4}{5}(155)$	Substitute -2 for v and 155 for w
		$6(-8) + \frac{4}{5}(155)$	Exponents
		$-48 + \frac{4}{5}(155)$	Multiply
		$-48 + 124$	Multiply
		76	Add
2	B	$\frac{6}{d} - 10c - c^4$	Original equation
		$\frac{6}{2} - 10(-3) - (-3)^4$	Substitute -3 for c and 2 for d
		$\frac{6}{2} - 10(-3) - (81)$	Exponents
		$3 - 10(-3) - (81)$	Divide
		$3 - (-30) - (81)$	Multiply
		$3 + 30 - (81)$	Change to adding
		$33 - (81)$	Add
		-48	Subtract
3	C	$V = s^3$	Formula
		$V = s^3$	Substitute 2 for s
		$V = 8 \text{ cm}^3$	Exponents
4	B	40, because 30 x 40 = 1200	
		Alternative Solution:	
		1200 / x = 30	
		x = 1200 / 30	
		x = 40	

6.EE.A.3 Writing Equivalent Expressions

Question No.	Answer	Detailed Explanation
1	B	Combine like terms in the expression. $u + u + u + u = 4u$ $-p + p + p = p$ That makes the equation $4u + p - r = 55$
2	B	The GCF of 36 and 12 is 12. The Distributive Property states that a number outside of the parentheses should be distributed to all numbers inside the parentheses. So, $36x - 12 = 108$ can be rewritten as $12(3x - 1) = 108$
3	B	The Distributive Property states that a number outside of the parentheses should be distributed to all numbers inside the parentheses. $5(3x + 2)$ $= (5*3x) + (5*2) = 15x + 10$.
4	C	First use the Distributive Property to remove the parentheses: $5b - 9c - 2(4b + c) = 5b - 9c - 8b - 2c$ Then, combine like terms: $5b - 9c - 8b - 2c = (5b - 8b) + (-9c - 2c) = -3b + (-11c) =$ $-3b - 11c$
5	(4 x 5) -3	(4 x 5) -3

6.EE.A.4 Identifying Equivalent Expressions

Question No.	Answer	Detailed Explanation
1	C	$(800 + 444y)/4$ and $200 + 111y$ are equivalent because if you divide $800 + 444y$ by 4 you will get $200 + 111y$. The expressions will be equivalent even if a number is substituted for y.
2	D	$5(19 - 8y)$ and $95 - 40y$ are equivalent because if you distribute 5 to $19 - 8y$ you will get $95 - 40y$. The expressions will be equivalent even if a number is substituted for y.
3	D	$3(26p - 7 + 14h)$ and $78p - 21 + 42h$ are equivalent because if you distribute 3 to $26p - 7 + 14h$ you will get $78p - 21 + 42h$. The expressions will be equivalent even if numbers are substituted for h and p.
4	12 y	$8y + 8y + 8y = 24y$. Therefore given expression $= 24y/2 = (24/2)y = 12y$.

6.EE.B.5 Equations and Inequalities

Question No.	Answer	Detailed Explanation
1	A	"The square of the sum of 6 and b" means to square all of $(6 + b)$, or $(6 + b)^2$ "is greater than 10" means "> 10" $(6 + b)^2 > 10$
2	B	"16 less than" means to "subtract 16 from some term" "the product of 5 and h" means to multiply 5 and h or "5h" "is 21" means "equals 21" $5h - 16 = 21$
3	C	"8 times the quantity $2x - 7$" means to multiply 8 and $2x - 7$, which needs to be in parentheses (as a quantity), so $8(2x - 7)$ "is greater than" means "$>$" 5 times the quantity $3x + 9$" means 5 multiplied by $3x + 9$, which needs to be in parentheses (as a quantity), so $5(3x+9)$ $8(2x - 7) > 5(3x + 9)$
4	A	5 because $3 \times 5 = 15$; $15 + 4$ is > 17.

6.EE.B.6 Modeling with Expressions

Question No.	Answer	Detailed Explanation
1	B	Janie started with 54 stamps. Giving t stamps away means $-t$, so $54 - t$. Then, Janie gets double t stamps back or $+ 2t$. $54 - t + 2t$. Simplified, the expression would be $54 + t$.
2	B	The director wants to buy double of x books, which is 2x. Add that to the 2,500 existing books to create the expression $2,500 + 2x$.
3	C	The total number of cupcakes is "c." There are 24 boys and 29 girls plus Claire (to make 30). Add all of the people together and equate it to "c." $24 + 30 = c$
4	C	Answer is $43 > q$ is the only choice that models a number "greater than" q.

6.EE.B.7 Solving One-Step Equations

Question No.	Answer	Detailed Explanation
1	A	$\frac{z}{5} = 20$ To find the value of z, you must isolate it. Multiply each side by 5/1 to cancel out the denominator and isolate the z. z/5 * 5/1 = z 20 * 5/1 = 100 so, z = 100
2	C	$\frac{y}{3} = 12$ To find the value of y, you must isolate it. Multiply by 3 on each side to isolate the y. y/3*(3/1) = 12(3/1) y = 36
3	B	To find the value of p, you must isolate it. Subtract 13 from both sides to isolate the variable. 13 + p − 13 = 39 − 13 p = 26
4	D	To find the value of w, you must isolate it. Divide each side by the coefficient, 6, to isolate the variable. 6w/6 = 54/6 w = 9
5	A	To find the value of m, you must isolate it. Divide both the sides by 4. 4m / 4 = 16 / 4 m = 4

6.EE.B.8 Representing Inequalities

Question No.	Answer	Detailed Explanation
1	C	"A number times six plus three" is represented as 6x + 3. Three times that is represented as 3(6x + 3). "Is less than" is represented as <. 3(6x + 3) < 27
2	B	An open circle means that the number the circle is over is not included in the answer. An arrow pointing to the right means "greater than". The number line would show an open circle over three with an arrow pointing to the right.
3	A	The number of jellybeans that Joey has is represented as x. Amy has three times that many so that is represented as 3x. Together they have at least 44. That means that their jellybeans added together are at least 44, so that is represented as x + 3x. At least means that they could have 44 or more than 44 so that is represented as ≥. x + 3x ≥ 44
4		"A number" is represented as x. "Divided by 5" is represented as $\frac{x}{5}$. "Is at most" means that it could be -23 or less than -23, so that is represented as ≤ $\frac{x}{5} \leq -23$

6.EE.C.9 Quantitative Relationships

Question No.	Answer	Detailed Explanation
1	C	"b" represents the number of bottles of lemonade "o" represents the total number of ounces of lemonade To find out the total number of ounces of lemonade that Penny purchased, multiply the number of bottles (b) by the number of ounces in each bottle, 60. 60(b) = o
2	B	"t" represents the total number of minutes Ethan played "g" represents the number of games "m" represent the number of minutes in each game To find out the total number of minutes Ethan played, multiply the number of games by the number of minutes in each game. t = g(m)
3	D	The equation t = c(n) can be used with any numbers. The equation has the number of trees and the cost of one tree as variables. Those quantities, no matter what they are, when multiplied together will always equal the total cost.
4		(see table and work below)

Day	Money Spent on Sodas	Sodas Purchased	Price per Soda
Monday	$30.00	24	$1.25
Wednesday	$57.50	46	$1.25
Friday	$41.25	33	$1.25

m = $30.00
24 x $1.25 = $30
w = 46 sodas
$57.50 / $1.25 = 46
f = 33 sodas
$41.25/ $1.25 = 33

Geometry

6.G.A.1 Area

1. The figure shows a small square inside a larger square. What is the area of the shaded portion of the figure below?

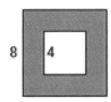

Ⓐ 64 square units
Ⓑ 48 square units
Ⓒ 16 square units
Ⓓ 80 square units

2. What is the area of the figure below?

7

7 ☐

Ⓐ 14 square units
Ⓑ 28 square units
Ⓒ 49 square units
Ⓓ 21 square units

3. What is the area of the figure below? (Assume that the vertical height of the triangle is 2.8 units)

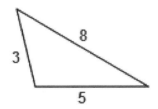

Ⓐ 15 square units
Ⓑ 7 square units
Ⓒ 14 square units
Ⓓ 40 square units

4. **Calculate the area of the triangle shown below and write the answer in the box.**

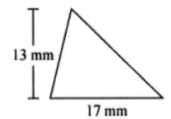

mm²

6.G.A.2 Surface Area and Volume

1. **Calculate the surface area of the box shown below.**

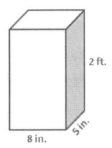

2 ft.

8 in.   5 in.

  Ⓐ 132 square inches
  Ⓑ 80 square inches
  Ⓒ 704 square inches
  Ⓓ 352 square inches

2. **Complete the following statement.**
   A hexagon must have _____.

  Ⓐ 6 sides and 6 angles
  Ⓑ 8 sides and 8 angles
  Ⓒ 10 sides and 10 angles
  Ⓓ 7 sides and 7 angles

3. **A single marble tile measures 25 cm by 20 cm. How many tiles will be required to cover a floor with dimensions 2 meters by 3 meters?**

  Ⓐ 320 tiles
  Ⓑ 240 tiles
  Ⓒ 180 tiles
  Ⓓ 120 tiles

4. **What is the volume of a rectangular prism that has a length of 10 cm, a width of 5 cm, and a height of 2 cm? Circle the correct answer choice.**

Ⓐ V = 50 cubic cm
Ⓑ V = 17 cubic cm
Ⓒ V = 10 cubic cm
Ⓓ V = 100 cubic cm

6.G.A.3 Coordinate Geometry

1. **Which of the following graphs shows a 180-degree clockwise rotation about the origin?**

Ⓐ
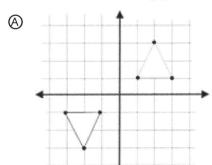

Ⓑ
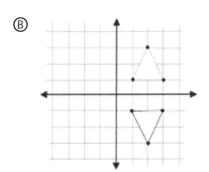

Ⓒ
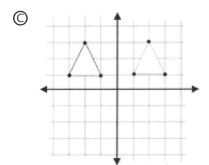

Ⓓ
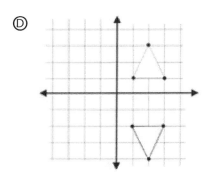

2. Identify the point on the grid below that corresponds to the ordered pair of x = 2y + 3, when y = 2.

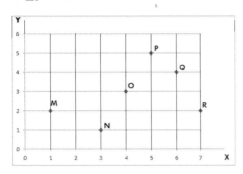

Ⓐ Point M
Ⓑ Point N
Ⓒ Point R
Ⓓ Point Q

3. Which figure is formed when you draw straight line segments between the following points (in the order they are listed)? (2, −13), (2, 1), (8, 1), (8, 5), (2, 5), (2, 10), (−2, 10), (−2, 5), (−8, 5), (−8, 1), (−2, 1), (−2, −13)

Ⓐ star
Ⓑ cross
Ⓒ heart
Ⓓ boat

4. What is the area of this polygon? Write your answer in the box given below.

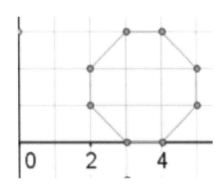

square units

6.G.A.4 Nets

1. Identify the solid given its net:

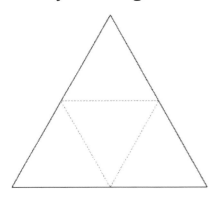

Ⓐ Cube
Ⓑ Sphere
Ⓒ Rectangular prism
Ⓓ Triangular pyramid

2. Identify the solid given its net:

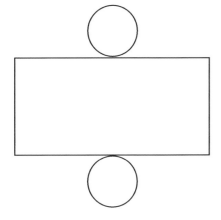

Ⓐ Cube
Ⓑ Sphere
Ⓒ Cylinder
Ⓓ Square pyramid

3. Identify the solid given its net:

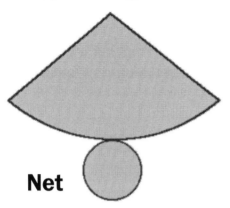

Net

Ⓐ Cube
Ⓑ Cone
Ⓒ Cylinder
Ⓓ Square pyramid

4. Use a net or formula to find the surface area of the figure. The length is 5, the width is 4 and the height is 2. Write your answer in the box given below.

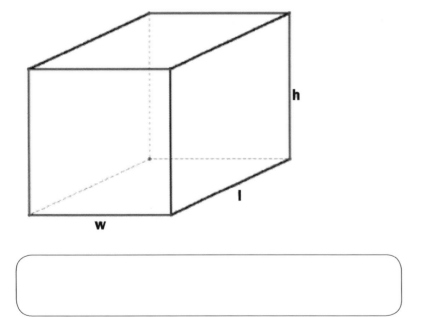

```
┌─────────────────────────────────────────────────┐
│                                                   │
│                                                   │
└─────────────────────────────────────────────────┘
```

Geometry

Answer Key
&
Detailed Explanations

6.G.A.1 Area

Question No.	Answer	Detailed Explanation
1	B	First find the area of the larger square. Then find the area of the smaller square. Use the formula: A = (length of side)² to find the area of both squares. $A_{large} = 8 \times 8 = 64$ $A_{small} = 4 \times 4 = 16$ Subtract the area of the smaller square from the larger square to find the area of the shaded portion (64 − 16 = 48).
2	C	Area of a square A = (length of side)² $A = 7^2$ A = 49 units²
3	B	Area of a triangle = (1/2)bh $A = (\frac{1}{2})(5*2.8)$ $A = (\frac{1}{2})(14)$ A = 7 units²
4	110.5 mm²	For a triangle, Area = ½ (base x height) b = 17 mm h = 13 mm So, ½ (17 x 13) = area ½ (221) = 110.5 mm²

6.G.A.2 Surface Area and Volume

Question No.	Answer	Detailed Explanation
1	C	First convert 2 feet to inches. There are 12 inches per foot so 2 feet is 12 * 2 = 24 inches. The given figure is a cuboid or a rectangular prism which has six rectangular surfaces. Area of a rectangle = length x breadth. Therefore total S.A. = $2(L_1W_1) + 2(L_2W_2) + 2(L_3W_3)$ where $L_1 W_1$ are the dimensions of the top and bottom faces of the prism; $L_2 W_2$ are the dimensions of the front and back faces of the prism and $L_3 W_3$ are the dimensions of the side faces of the prism. Replace the variables with the appropriate values: S.A. = 2(5*8) + 2(8*24) + 2(5*24) S.A. = 2(40) + 2(192) + 2(120) S.A. = 80 + 384 + 240 S.A. = 704 square inches
2	A	A hexagon is a shape with 6 angles and 6 sides.
3	D	First, convert meters into centimeters to standardize the measurement units. 1 meter = 100 centimeters, so 2 meters = 200 centimeters and 3 meters = 300 centimeters. To find how many tiles will be needed across, divide $\frac{300}{25} = 12$ To find how many tiles will be needed down, divide $\frac{200}{20} = 10$ Then multiply the number of tiles needed across the floor by the number of times needed down the floor. 12*10 = 120 tiles.
4	D	V = LWH V = (10)(5)(2) V = 50(2) V = 100 cubic cm

6.G.A.3 Coordinate Geometry

Question No.	Answer	Detailed Explanation
1	A	A 180-degree clockwise rotation about the origin will cause the top of the triangle to point to the bottom, and also the shape to shift from Quadrant I to Quadrant III.
2	C	$x = 2y + 3$, when $y = 2$ Substitute 2 for y. $x = 2(2) + 3$ $x = 4 + 3$ $x = 7$ This makes the ordered pair (7,2), which corresponds to point R.
3	B	 When all points are correctly plotted, a cross is formed.
4	7 square units.	7 square units. There are 5 whole square units. There are 4 units that are right triangles, for a total of 2 whole squares. $5 + 2 = 7$ square units.

6.G.A.4 Nets

Question No.	Answer	Detailed Explanation
1	D	When the exposed edges are connected a triangular pyramid will be formed.
2	C	When the exposed edges are connected a cylinder will be formed.
3	B	When the exposed edges are connected a cone will be formed.
4	C	To find the surface area, find the area of each side using the net S.A. = (5*4) + (5*4) + (4*2) + (4*2) + (5*2) + (5*2) = = 20 + 20 + 8 + 8 + 10 + 10 = 76 square units

Statistics & Probability

6.SP.A.1 Statistical Questions

1. **Goldie wants to find out how many presents children get for their birthdays. She surveys 11 families in the same neighborhood to find out how many presents their children get. Did Goldie get a representative sample?**

   Ⓐ No because she did not ask the right questions.
   Ⓑ No because she asked families in the same neighborhood who most likely have similar income levels.
   Ⓒ Yes because she asked families in the same neighborhood who most likely have similar income levels.
   Ⓓ Yes because she asked the right questions.

2. **Roberta is an arborist. She is studying maple trees in a specific area. Roberta wants to show a class the difference in the heights of the trees so that they can compare them. What type of graph would be best for that?**

   Ⓐ Line graph
   Ⓑ Picture graph
   Ⓒ Circle graph
   Ⓓ Bar graph

3. **Derek spends an average of 37 minutes a weekday on homework. He wants to know how much time other students in fourth grade spend on homework so he asks only students in his class. Will Derek's survey be biased?**

   Ⓐ Yes because he is asking fourth graders.
   Ⓑ No because he is asking fourth graders.
   Ⓒ Yes because students in his class have the same amount of homework as he does.
   Ⓓ No because students in his class have the same amount of homework as he does.

4. **Select the questions that qualify as statistical questions. Choose all that apply.**

   Ⓐ How many letters are in my last name?
   Ⓑ How many letters are in the last names of the students in my 6th grade class?
   Ⓒ What are the colors of the shoes worn by the students in my school?
   Ⓓ What are the heart rates of the students in a 6th grade class?
   Ⓔ How many hours of sleep per night do 6th graders usually get when they have school the next day?

1. A .J. has downloaded 400 songs onto his computer. The songs are from a variety of genres. The circle graph below shows the breakdown (by genre) of his collection. Use the information shown to respond to the following: About how many more R + B songs than rock songs has A.J. downloaded?

A.J.'s Music Collections

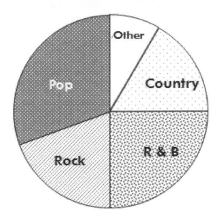

   Ⓐ 20 more songs
   Ⓑ 30 more songs
   Ⓒ 50 more songs
   Ⓓ 75 more songs

2. Colleen has to travel for work. In one week, she traveled all five work days. The shortest distance she traveled was 63 miles. The range of miles that she traveled was 98 miles. What is the longest distance that Colleen traveled for work in one week?

   Ⓐ 161 miles
   Ⓑ 98 miles
   Ⓒ 33 miles
   Ⓓ It cannot be determined.

3. Bob is a mailman. He delivers a lot of letters every day. His mail bag will only hold so many letters. The most letters that Bob has ever delivered in a day is 8,476. The range of the number of letters that Bob has ever delivered is 6,930. What is the least number of letters that Bob has ever delivered in one day?

   Ⓐ 15,406 letters
   Ⓑ 1,546 letters
   Ⓒ 1,556 letters
   Ⓓ It cannot be determined.

4. The height of the four tallest downtown buildings of three different cities is given in the table below. Calculate the mean height of each city's buildings and match it with the correct answer from the bottom table.

City A Buildings	Height (m)
1	23
2	32
3	35
4	45

City B Buildings	Height (m)
1	15
2	22
3	28
4	25

City C Buildings	Height (m)
1	15
2	30
3	35
4	36

	22.50 m	29 m	23.20 m	33.75 m	18 m
City A Buildings	◯	◯	◯	◯	◯
City B Buildings	◯	◯	◯	◯	◯
City C Buildings	◯	◯	◯	◯	◯

6.SP.A.3 Central Tendency

1. **A = { 10, 15, 2, 14, 19, 25, 0 }**

   Which of the following numbers, if added to Set A, would have the greatest effect on its median?

   Ⓐ 14
   Ⓑ 50
   Ⓒ 5
   Ⓓ 15

2. **What is the mean, median and mode for the following data?**

   {−7, 18, 29, 4, −3, 11, 22}

   Ⓐ Mean = 10
       Median = 18
       Mode = −3

   Ⓑ Mean = 11
       Median = 11
       Mode = none

   Ⓒ Mean = 10.57
       Median = 11
       Mode = none

   Ⓓ Mean = 10
       Median = 18
       Mode = −3

3. **Amanda had the following numbers: 1, 2, 6**

   If she added the number 3 to the list...

   Ⓐ the mean would increase
   Ⓑ the mean would decrease
   Ⓒ the median would increase
   Ⓓ the median would decrease

4. **Select the median number for each set of numbers.**

	3	4	8
4, 2, 3, 6, 4, 9, 7	O	O	O
6, 3, 2, 8, 1, 3, 6	O	O	O
8, 9, 4, 8, 1, 10, 3	O	O	O

6.SP.B.4 Graphs & Charts

1. The results of the class' most recent science test are displayed in this histogram. Use the results to answer the question.

   What percentage of the class scored an 81-90 on the test?

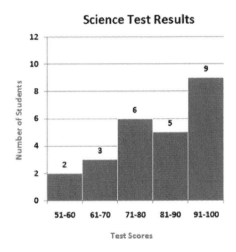

Science Test Results

   Ⓐ 5%
   Ⓑ 20%
   Ⓒ 25%
   Ⓓ 30%

2. How much of the graph do undergarments and socks make up together?

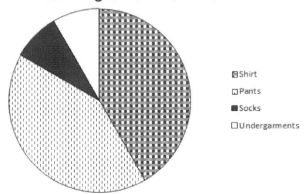

Clothing Sales Breakdown

☒ Shirt
☐ Pants
■ Socks
☐ Undergarments

   Ⓐ less than 5%
   Ⓑ between 5% and 10%
   Ⓒ between 10% and 25%
   Ⓓ more than 25%

3. As part of their weather unit, the students in Mr. Green's class prepared a line graph show-ing the high and low temperatures recorded each day during a one-week period. Use the graph to answer the question.

    What percentage of the days had a temperature 80 degrees or higher? Round to the nearest tenth.

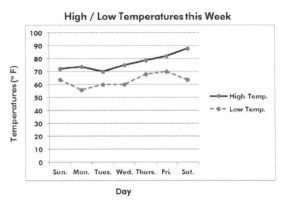

    Ⓐ 14.3%
    Ⓑ 42.9%
    Ⓒ 28.6%
    Ⓓ None of these

Refer below bar graph to answer the following question.

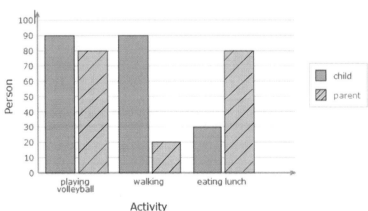

4. What is the total number of parents and children who played volleyball and ate lunch? Write your answer in the box below.

6.SP.B.5.B Describing the Nature

1. **Terry is playing a game with his brother and they played 5 times. The median score that Terry got was 37. The range of Terry's scores was 40. What was the lowest and highest score that Terry got?**

   Ⓐ 37 and 77
   Ⓑ 10 and 50
   Ⓒ 17 and 57
   Ⓓ Not enough information is given.

2. **Marcus wants to find out how many people go to the zoo on Saturdays in August. The zoo is open for 7 hours and there are 4 Saturdays in August. He counts the number of people who enter the zoo for two hours one Saturday. Will Marcus get an accurate idea of how many people go to the zoo?**

   Ⓐ Yes because he will get a good representative sample.
   Ⓑ No because he will not get enough of a representative sample.
   Ⓒ Yes because he can assume that two hours is enough time to count the number of people.
   Ⓓ No because he would need to be there for less time.

3. **Carl surveys his class to find out how tall his classmates are.**
   How many classmates did Carl survey?

Height	Number of Classmates
4'4" – 4'8"	1
4'9" – 5'	4
5'1" – 5'5"	7
5'6" – 5'11"	14
6' – 6'4"	2

   Ⓐ 27
   Ⓑ 28
   Ⓒ 14
   Ⓓ 24

4. **What is the mean of these numbers? 5, 4, 3, 7, 8, 9. Circle the correct answer choice.**

   Ⓐ 6
   Ⓑ 5
   Ⓒ 7
   Ⓓ 3

6.SP.B.5.C Context of Data Gathered

1. **What is the mean absolute deviation of the grades Charlene received on her first ten quizzes:**
   83%, 92%, 76%, 87%, 89%, 96%, 88%, 91%, 79%, 99%.

   Ⓐ 4.5%
   Ⓑ 5.4%
   Ⓒ 88%
   Ⓓ 88.5%

2. **The following numbers are the minutes it took Nyak to complete one lap around a certain dirt bike course. What is the mean absolute deviation of this data set?**

   12.3, 12.6, 12.2, 10.9, 11.3, 10.3, 11.7, 10.7

   Ⓐ 0.7 minutes
   Ⓑ 0.75 minutes
   Ⓒ 11.1 minutes
   Ⓓ 1.5 minutes

3. **The local Akita Rescue Organization has nine Akitas for adoption. Their weights are 82 lbs, 95 lbs, 130 lbs, 112 lbs, 122 lbs, 72 lbs, 86, lbs, 145 lbs, 93 lbs. What are the median (M), 1st Quartile (Q1), 3rd Quartile (Q3) and Interquartile Range (IQR) of this data set?**

   Ⓐ M = 95, Q1 = 84, Q3 = 126, IQR = 42
   Ⓑ M = 95, Q1 = 85, Q3 = 126, IQR = 145
   Ⓒ M = 95, Q1 = 84, Q3 = 145, IQR = 42
   Ⓓ M = 95, Q1 = 126, Q3 = 145, IQR = 42

4. **Frank played 9 basketball games this season. His scores were 15, 20, 14, 36, 20, 10, 35, 23 and 24. What is the median of Frank's scores? Write the answer in the box.**

6.SP.B.5.D Relating Data Distributions

1. The frequency table below records the age of the student who attended the dance.

Age	Frequency
11	17
12	20
13	9
14	8
15	12
16	4

Which of the following statements is true based on this data?

Ⓐ 80 students attended the dance.
Ⓑ The mean age is 12.86
Ⓒ If 3 more 16-year-olds arrive, the median age would increase.
Ⓓ More than half the students are older than the mean.

2. For twelve weeks Jeb has recorded his car's fuel mileage in miles per gallon (mpg). He has plotted these fuel mileages below in a box plot.

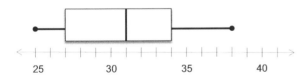

25   30   35   40

Which of the following statements is true based on this data?

Ⓐ The best fuel mileage recorded was 34 mpg.
Ⓑ Half of the data collected was between 27 mpg and 34 mpg.
Ⓒ The median fuel mileage was 30.5 mpg.
Ⓓ Three data points lie in the Interquartile range.

3. **"Forever Green"** recorded the heights of the pine trees sold this month in the box plot shown below. There are 15 data points in Quartile 3.

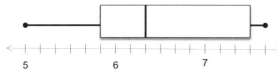

5   6   7

Which of the following statements is true based on this data?

Ⓐ About 25% of the trees were 7 feet 3 inches or taller.
Ⓑ There are more data points in Quartile 2 than Quartile 3.
Ⓒ The median height is 6 feet 2 inches.
Ⓓ "Forever Green" sold a total of about 60 trees this month.

4. Three volleyball teams each recorded their scores for their first 5 games. Use each team's scores below to determine the missing value.

	10	14	17
Team 1: 15, 16, t, 17, 12, Mode = 17, What is t?	○	○	○
Team 2: 7, 14, r, 16, 13 Mean = 12, What is r?	○	○	○
Team 3: 11, 7, 19, 14, z, Median = 14, What is z?	○	○	○

6.SP.B.5 Data Interpretation

1. There are three ice cream stands within 15 miles and they are owned by Mr. Sno.

Ice Cream Stand	Vanilla	Chocolate	Twist
A	15	22	10
B	24	8	14
C	20	16	13

   What percentage of the ice cream cones sold by Ice Cream Stand C were chocolate? Round your answer to the nearest whole number.

   Ⓐ 30%
   Ⓑ 32%
   Ⓒ 33%
   Ⓓ 62%

2. Alexander plays baseball. His batting averages for the games he played this year were recorded. What is the batting average he had the most often?

   {.228, .316, .225, .333, .228, .125, .750, .500}

   Ⓐ .228
   Ⓑ .316
   Ⓒ .750
   Ⓓ .333

3. How much will the mean increase by when the number 17 is added to the set? Round your numbers to the nearest tenth.

   {5, -10, 14, 6, 8, -2, 11, 3, 6}

   Ⓐ 1.5
   Ⓑ 1
   Ⓒ 1.2
   Ⓓ 1.7

4. Scientists were concerned about the survival of the Mississippi Blue Catfish, so they collected data from samples of this species of fish. The scientists captured the fish, measured them, and then returned them to the lake from which they were taken. Select the correct numbers for different ranges of lengths.

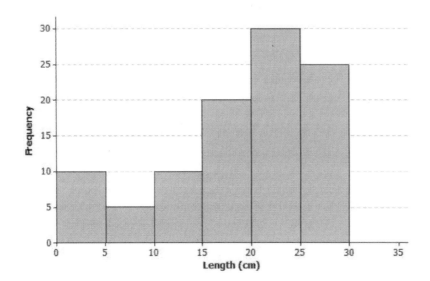

	5	10	20	25	30
0 – <5 cm	O	O	O	O	O
5 – <10 cm	O	O	O	O	O
10 – <15 cm	O	O	O	O	O
15 – <20 cm	O	O	O	O	O
20 – <25 cm	O	O	O	O	O

Statistics & Probability

Answer Key
&
Detailed Explanations

6.SP.A.1 Statistical Questions

Question No.	Answer	Detailed Explanation
1	B	A representative sample should be a sample of people who represent the larger population. Surveying all families in one neighborhood would not be representative because people in the same neighborhood most likely have the same income level.
2	D	A bar graph would be best because it shows the data in bars that are then very easy to compare.
3	C	Derek's survey will be biased because the students in his class have the same amount of homework as he does. To get an unbiased sample, he should ask students from all fourth grade classes.
4	B, C, D & E	Options (B), (C), (D), and (E) are correct, A statistical question is one that can be answered by collecting data that vary (i.e., not all of the data values are the same).

6.SP.A.2 Distribution

Question No.	Answer	Detailed Explanation
1	A	Angle corresponding to R + B songs = 90 degrees. The number of R + B songs downloaded is $400 \times (\frac{90}{360}) = 400 \times (\frac{1}{4}) = 100$ songs ($\frac{90}{360} = \frac{1}{4}$ after taking GCF 90 out of both the numerator and denominator) Angle correspoding to rock songs is close to 90 degrees but less than 90 degrees. Let us take it to be 75 degrees (approximately) So, number of rock songs downloaded is $400 \times (\frac{75}{360}) = 400 \times (\frac{5}{24}) = 83$ (approximately) ($\frac{75}{360} = \frac{5}{24}$ after taking GCF 15 out of both the numerator and denominator) Therefore A.J. has downloaded 100 - 83 = 17 more R + B songs than rock songs. Among the choices given, (A) is the most appropriate choice.
2	A	To find the longest distance Colleen traveled, add the shortest distance to the range. 63 + 98 = 161

Question No.	Answer	Detailed Explanation
3	B	To find the least number of letters that Bob has ever delivered, subtract the range from the largest number. 8,476 − 6,930 = 1,546 letters
4		City A = 33.75m City B = 22.50 m City C = 29 m Find the sum of the height of all four buildings and divide by 4 to determine the mean.

6.SP.A.3 Central Tendency

Question No.	Answer	Detailed Explanation
1	C	0, 2, 10, 14, 15, 19, 25 Median is 14. (A) If 14 is added to the set, median = 14. So, it does not change. (B) If 50 is added to the set, median $= \dfrac{14+15}{2} = 14.5$. So, median increases by 0.5. (C) If 5 is added to the set, median $= \dfrac{10+14}{2} = 12$. So, median decreases by 2. (D) If 15 is added to the set, median $= \dfrac{14+15}{2} = 14.5$. So, median increases by 0.5. Therefore, median would be affected most by adding the score 5 to the set. Option (C) is the correct answer.
2	C	{−7, 18, 29, 4, −3, 11, 22} There is no mode because no numbers repeat To find the median, list the numbers in order from smallest to largest. −7, −3, 4, 11, 18, 22, 29 The median = 11. To find the average, add all of the numbers together and divide by 7. $\dfrac{-7 + 18 + 29 + 4 + (-3) + 11 + 22}{7} = x$ x = 10.57

Question No.	Answer	Detailed Explanation
3	C	Mean for original set: $1 + 2 + 6 = 9$ $\frac{9}{3} = 3$ Median for original set: 2 Mean after adding 3: $1 + 2 + 3 + 6 = 12$ $\frac{12}{4} = 3$ Median after adding 3: $2 + 3 = 5$ $\frac{5}{2} = 2.5$

4			3	4	8
		4, 2, 3, 6, 4, 9, 7		◯	
		6, 3, 2, 8, 1, 3, 6	◯		
		8, 9, 4, 8, 1, 10, 3			◯

To determine the median number, first, order the set of numbers from least to greatest. The median number will be the number in the center.

6.SP.B.4 Graphs & Charts

Question No.	Answer	Detailed Explanation
1	B	5 students scored an 81-90 on the test out of 25 students. Convert this fraction into percentage. 5/25 * 100 = 20%
2	C	Socks and undergarments together appear to take up more than a tenth, but less than a quarter, of the pie chart. The percentage would be between 10% and 25%.
3	C	Friday and Saturday both had temperatures of 80 degrees or higher. That means that $\frac{2}{7}$ days were 80 degrees or more. Convert $\frac{2}{7}$ into percentage by multiplying $\frac{2}{7}$ with 100. $\frac{2}{7}$ x 100 = 28.57% Round to the nearest tenth making the percentage 28.6%
4	280	Parents volleyball: 80 Children volleyball: 90 Parents lunch: 80 Children lunch: 30 **Total:** **280**

6.SP.B.5.B Describing the Nature

Question No.	Answer	Detailed Explanation
1	D	Just knowing the median and the range is not enough information to figure out the lowest and highest scores.
2	B	In order to get a representative sample, the person who is conducting the survey needs to get a good sample of what they are surveying. Marcus would need to spend more than 2 hours at the zoo to get a good sample. He should also go on more than one Saturday.
3	B	To figure out how many classmates Carl surveyed, add together all of the numbers in the "Number of Classmates" column. $1 + 4 + 7 + 14 + 2 = 28$
4	A	The numbers added together equal 36, and $36/6 = 6$

6.SP.B.5.C Context of Data Gathered

Question No.	Answer	Detailed Explanation
1	B	First find the mean. $\dfrac{83 + 92 + 76 + 87 + 89 + 96 + 88 + 91 + 79 + 99}{10} = \dfrac{880}{10} = 88\%$ Now find the distance between each number and the average. $\|83-88\|=5$ $\|92-88\|=4$ $\|76-88\|=12$ $\|87-88\|=1$ $\|89-88\|=1$ $\|96-88\|=8$ $\|88-88\|=0$ $\|91-88\|=3$ $\|79-88\|=9$ $\|99-88\|=11$ Take the average of these differences $\dfrac{5 + 4 + 12 + 1 + 1 + 8 + 0 + 3 + 9 + 11}{10} = \dfrac{54}{10} = 5.4\%$

Question No.	Answer	Detailed Explanation
2	A	First find the mean. $$\frac{12.3 + 12.6 + 12.2 + 10.9 + 11.3 + 10.3 + 11.7 + 10.7}{8} = \frac{92}{8} = 11.5$$ Now find the distance between each number and the average. $\|12.3-11.5\|=0.8$ $\|12.6-11.5\|=1.1$ $\|12.2-11.5\|=0.7$ $\|10.9-11.5\|=0.6$ $\|11.3-11.5\|=0.2$ $\|10.3-11.5\|=1.2$ $\|11.7-11.5\|=0.2$ $\|10.7-11.5\|=0.8$ Take the average of these differences $$\frac{0.8 + 1.1 + 0.7 + 0.6 + 0.2 + 1.2 + 0.2 + 0.8}{8} = \frac{5.6}{8} = 0.7 min$$
3	A	Put the numbers in order from least to greatest. 72 82 86 93 95 112 122 130 145 Median = 95 $Q1 = \frac{82 + 86}{2} = 84$ $Q3 = \frac{122 + 130}{2} = 126$ IQR = 126 − 84 = 42 M = 95, Q1 = 84, Q3 = 126, IQR = 42
4	20	To find the median score, order the numbers from least to greatest. 10, 14, 15, 20, 20, 23, 24, 35, 36 Then identify the number that is in the middle. In this list, 20 is in the middle of the list so the median is 20.

6.SP.B.5.D Relating Data Distributions

Question No.	Answer	Detailed Explanation
1	B	A) False. $17 + 20 + 9 + 8 + 12 + 4 = 70$ students
		B) True. $\frac{[17(11) + 20(12) + 9(13) + 8(14) + 12(15) + 4(16)]}{70} = \frac{900}{70} = 12.86$
		C) False. The current median age is the average of the 35th and 36th numbers which is $\frac{12 + 12}{2} = 12$. If three sixteen year olds arrived the median number would be the 37th number which is 12. Therefore the median age would not change.
		D) False. There are 33 students older than the mean of 12.86. Half of 70 would be 35 and 33 is less than 35. Therefore less than half of the students are older than the mean.
2	B	A) False. The best fuel mileage recorded was 38 mpg.
		B) True. The Interquartile range is from $27 - 34$ mpg which contains 50% of the data.
		C) False. The median fuel mileage was 31 mpg.
		D) False. There are twelve data points in all which means that each quartile contains four points and the IQR contains two quartiles or eight points.
3	D	Note: Each tick mark is 2 inches.
		A) False. About 25% of the trees were 7 feet 6 inches or taller.
		B) False. Each quartile has the same number of data points.
		C) False. The median height is 6 feet 4 inches.
		D) True. If Q3 has 15 data points then so do Q1, Q2 and Q4. This makes a total of $15 * 4 = 60$ trees. We say "about" because the median may not be in a quartile.

Question No.	Answer	Detailed Explanation

Question No. 4 — **Answer: C**

	10	14	17
Team 1: 15, 16, t, 17, 12, Mode = 17, What is t?			●
Team 2: 7, 14, r, 16, 13 Mean = 12, What is r?	●		
Team 3: 11, 7, 19, 14, z, Median = 14, What is z?		●	

Team 1: t=17 would be the mode because it would be listed two times.
Team 2: (7 + 14 + r + 16 + 13) / 5 = 12
      (50 + r) = 12 x 5 = 60
      r = 60 - 50 = 10
Team 3: Arrange the known numbers in ascending order : 7, 11, 14, 19. It is given median is 14. Therefore, the unknown number z must be more than or equal to 14. z = 14

6.SP.B.5 Data Interpretation

Question No.	Answer	Detailed Explanation
1	C	To figure out the percentage, add together all of the ice cream cones sold by stand C. 20 + 16 + 13 = 49 To find the percentage, divide 16 by 49 16/49 = .327 (when rounded to the nearest thousandth) To make the decimal into a percentage, move the decimal point to the right two places and round up. 33%
2	A	The number that shows up most often is the mode. .228 is the mode.
3	C	To find the mean, add all of the numbers together and divide by 9. 5 + -10 +14 + 6 +8 +-2 +11 + 3 + 6 = 41 41 ÷ 9 ≈ 4.6 (when rounded to the nearest tenth) 5 + -10 +14 + 6 +8 +-2 +11 + 3 + 6 + 17 = 58 58 ÷ 10 = 5.8 When 17 is added, the mean is 5.8 5.8 - 4.6 = 1.2
4		(see table below)

	5	10	20	25	30
0 – <5 cm		O			
5 – <10 cm	O				
10 – <15 cm		O			
15 – <20 cm			O		
20 – <25 cm					O

Additional Information

What if I buy more than one Lumos Study Program?

Step 1	**Visit the URL and login to your account.** http://www.lumoslearning.com
Step 2	Click on 'My tedBooks' under the "Account" tab. Place the Book Access Code and submit.

Step 3   To add the new book for a registered student, choose the
○ Existing Student button and select the student and submit.

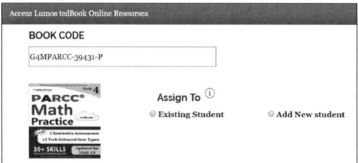

To add the new book for a new student, choose the ○ Add New student
button and complete the student registration.

Lumos StepUp® Mobile App FAQ For Students

What is the Lumos StepUp® App?

It is a FREE application you can download onto your Android Smartphones, tablets, iPhones, and iPads.

What are the Benefits of the StepUp® App?

This mobile application gives convenient access to Practice Tests, Common Core State Standards, Online Workbooks, and learning resources through your Smartphone and tablet computers.

- Eleven Technology enhanced question types in both MATH and ELA
- Sample questions for Arithmetic drills
- Standard specific sample questions
- Instant access to the Common Core State Standards
- Jokes and cartoons to make learning fun!

Do I Need the StepUp® App to Access Online Workbooks?

No, you can access Lumos StepUp® Online Workbooks through a personal computer. The StepUp® app simply enhances your learning experience and allows you to conveniently access StepUp® Online Workbooks and additional resources through your smartphone or tablet.

How can I Download the App?

Visit **lumoslearning.com/a/stepup-app** using your Smartphone or tablet and follow the instructions to download the app.

**QR Code
for Smartphone
Or Tablet Users**

Lumos StepUp® Mobile App FAQ For Parents and Teachers

What is the Lumos StepUp® App?

It is a free app that teachers can use to easily access real-time student activity information as well as assign learning resources to students. Parents can also use it to easily access school-related information such as homework assigned by teachers and PTA meetings. It can be downloaded onto smartphones and tablets from popular App Stores.

What are the Benefits of the Lumos StepUp® App?

It provides convenient access to

- Standards aligned learning resources for your students
- An easy to use Dashboard
- Student progress reports
- Active and inactive students in your classroom
- Professional development information
- Educational Blogs

How can I Download the App?

Visit **lumoslearning.com/a/stepup-app** using your Smartphone or tablet and follow the instructions to download the app.

QR Code
for Smartphone
Or Tablet Users

Lumos Back-to-School Refresher tedBook - 7th Grade English Language Arts,
Back to School book to address Summer Slide designed for classroom and home use

GRADE 6 ≫ 7

BACK TO SCHOOL
REFRESHER
ENGLISH
LANGUAGE ARTS

★ **Grade 6 Review**   ★ **Preview of Grade 7**

Measure and Remediate Learning Loss

Diagnose
Learning Gaps

Get Targeted
Practice

Prepare for
Grade 7

Updated for 2021-22

(((tedBook)))

Includes Additional Online Practice

Other Books By Lumos Learning For Grade 7

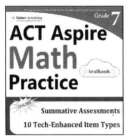 

ACT Aspire Math & ELA Practice Book

AzM2 Math & ELA Practice Book

CMAS Math & ELA Practice Book

FSA Math & ELA Practice Book

GMAS Math & ELA Practice Book

ILEARN Math & ELA Practice Book

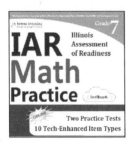 

IAR Math & ELA Practice Book

LEAP Math & ELA Practice Book